REFLE
ON
PS

IAN ADAMS
CHRISTOPHER COCKSWORTH
JOANNA COLLICUTT
GILLIAN COOPER
STEVEN CROFT
PAULA GOODER
PETER GRAYSTONE
MALCOLM GUITE
HELEN-ANN HARTLEY
BARBARA MOSSE
MARK OAKLEY
MARTYN PERCY
JOHN PRITCHARD
BEN QUASH
JOHN SENTAMU
ANGELA TILBY
LUCY WINKETT
JEREMY WORTHEN

Church House Publishing
Church House
Great Smith Street
London SW1P 3AZ

ISBN 978 0 7151 4490 9

Published 2015 by Church House Publishing
Copyright © The Archbishops' Council 2015

Liturgical editor: Peter Moger
Series editor: Hugh Hillyard-Parker
Designed and typeset by Hugh Hillyard-Parker
Copy edited by: Ros Connelly and Ruth Oakley
Printed by Ashford Colour Press Ltd

What do you think of *Reflections on the Psalms*?

We'd love to hear from you – simply email us at

publishing@churchofengland.org

or write to us at

Church House Publishing, Church House, Great Smith Street,
London SW1P 3AZ.

Visit **www.dailyprayer.org.uk** for more information on the
Reflections series, ordering and subscriptions.

Contents

About the authors

Ian Adams is a poet, writer, photographer and artist. He is the creator of the daily *Morning Bell*, author of *Unfurling:poems*, *Running Over Rocks: spiritual practices to transform tough times* and *Cave Refectory Road: monastic rhythms for contemporary living*. Ian is an Anglican priest, director of *StillPoint*, co-founder of *Beloved Life* and Spirituality Adviser for CMS. info: www.about.me/ianadams

Christopher Cocksworth is the Bishop of Coventry. He read Theology at the University of Manchester. After teaching in secondary education, he trained for ordination and pursued doctoral studies, serving in parochial and chaplaincy ministry and in theological education, latterly as Principal of Ridley Hall, Cambridge.

Joanna Collicutt is the Karl Jaspers Lecturer in Psychology and Spirituality at Ripon College Cuddesdon and Advisor on the Spiritual Care of Older People for Oxford Diocese. Her professional background is in clinical psychology, but her current area of academic interest is psychology of religion and, in particular, psychological approaches to reading the Bible. She also ministers in a West Oxfordshire parish.

Gillian Cooper is a writer, teacher, and Old Testament enthusiast. She has previously worked as a theological educator, a cathedral verger, and an administrator. She has recently moved to London, but still escapes whenever she can to the windswept beaches of Norfolk and Orkney.

Steven Croft is the Bishop of Sheffield. He is the author of a number of books including *Jesus People: what next for the church?* and *The Advent Calendar*, a novel for children and adults, and a co-author of *Pilgrim: a course for the Christian journey*.

Paula Gooder is Theologian in Residence for the Bible Society. She is a writer and lecturer in biblical studies, author of a number of books including *Journey to the Empty Tomb, The Meaning is in the Waiting* and *Heaven*, and a co-author of the Pilgrim course. She is also a Reader in the Church of England.

Peter Graystone works for Church Army, where he oversees pioneering projects that take the Good News way beyond the walls of a church to profoundly unchurched people. One of those locations is the internet, and he edits Christianity.org.uk, which gives free, confidential, reliable information about the Christian faith. He is a *Church Times* columnist and theatre reviewer.

Malcolm Guite, the Chaplain of Girton College, Cambridge, is a poet and singer–songwriter, and is the author of *What do Christians Believe?* (Granta 2006), *Faith, Hope and Poetry* (Ashgate 2010), *Sounding the Seasons: Seventy Sonnets for the Christian Year* (Canterbury 2012), *The Singing Bowl* (Canterbury 2013) and *Word in the Wilderness* (Canterbury 2014).

Helen-Ann Hartley is the 7th Bishop of Waikato in the Diocese of Waikato and Taranaki, New Zealand. Prior to her consecration, Helen-Ann was Dean at the College of St John the Evangelist in Auckland, New Zealand. She was ordained deacon and priest in the Diocese of Oxford and served as Director of Biblical Studies at Ripon College Cuddesdon prior to her move to New Zealand in 2012.

Barbara Mosse is a writer and retired Anglican priest. She was a lecturer on the MA in Christian Spirituality at Sarum College, Salisbury. Earlier ministerial posts included some parish work, alongside chaplaincy experience in prison, university, community mental health and hospital. She is the author of *The Treasures of Darkness* (Canterbury 2003), *Encircling the Christian Year* (BRF 2012) and *Welcoming the Way of the Cross* (BRF 2013).

Mark Oakley is Canon Chancellor of St Paul's Cathedral. A former Chaplain to the Bishop of London and Rector of St Paul's, Covent Garden, he is also the author of *The Collage of God* (2001) and various anthologies, including *Readings for Funerals* (2015), articles and reviews, usually in the areas of faith, poetry and literature. He is Visiting Lecturer in the department of Theology and Religious Studies at King's College London.

Martyn Percy is the Dean of Christ Church, Oxford, one of the University of Oxford's largest colleges, as well as the Cathedral Church of the diocese of Oxford. From 2004 to 2014 he was Principal of Ripon College, Cuddesdon. Prior to that he was Director of the Lincoln Theological Institute and has also been Chaplain and Director of Studies at Christ's College, Cambridge.

John Pritchard has recently retired as Bishop of Oxford. Prior to that he has been Bishop of Jarrow, Archdeacon of Canterbury and Warden of Cranmer Hall, Durham. His only ambition was to be a vicar, which he was in Taunton for eight happy years. He enjoys armchair sport, walking, reading, music, theatre and recovering.

Ben Quash has been Professor of Christianity and the Arts at King's College London since 2007, and is Director of the Centre for Arts and the Sacred at King's (ASK). Prior to that he was Dean and Fellow of Peterhouse, Cambridge. He runs a collaborative MA in Christianity and the Arts with the National Gallery in London, and is also Canon Theologian of both Coventry and Bradford Cathedrals.

John Sentamu practised Law both at the Bar and at the Bench in Uganda before he came to the UK in 1974. He was ordained priest in 1979, and was appointed Bishop for Stepney in 1996, Bishop for Birmingham in 2002 and Archbishop of York in 2005. He is Primate of England and Metropolitan, a member of the House of Lords and a Privy Councillor.

Angela Tilby is a Canon of Christ Church, Oxford and is Continuing Ministerial Development Adviser for the Diocese of Oxford. Prior to that she has been Vice-Principal of Westcott House, Cambridge and a senior producer at the BBC, where she made several acclaimed television programmes and series.

Lucy Winkett is Rector of St James's Church, Piccadilly. She contributes regularly to Radio 4's *Thought for the Day* and is the author of *Our Sound is our Wound* (Continuum 2010). She combines parish ministry with chairing an educational trust and running an all-through Church of England Academy, including a project for children on the autistic spectrum. Until 2010, she was Canon Precentor of St Paul's Cathedral.

Jeremy Worthen is a priest in the Church of England and is currently the Secretary for Ecumenical Relations and Theology at the Council for Christian Unity. He previously worked in theological education and has written on a range of subjects, including Jewish–Christian relations. His most recent book is *Responding to God's Call* (Canterbury Press 2012).

About *Reflections on the Psalms*

Reflections on the Psalms is a companion publication to the highly successful annual series of *Reflections for Daily Prayer*; this book offers a series of short reflections on each of the Psalms, written by a varied team of popular writers, experienced ministers, biblical scholars and theologians, all of whom bring their own emphases, enthusiasms and approaches to biblical interpretation to bear.

Regular users of *Morning Prayer* and *Time to Pray* (from *Common Worship: Daily Prayer*) will benefit from the rich variety of traditions represented in these stimulating and accessible pieces.

Unlike *Reflections for Daily Prayer* this volume is not tied to the annual lectionary; rather it will form a perpetual companion for Morning and/or Evening Prayer, and will also be a good reference for preaching from the principal service Lectionary readings, which always include a psalm.

As such this book will be a valuable resource for personal or devotional use. Some readers may use it in tandem with *Reflections for Daily Prayer*; others may choose to use it in place of it for a while. Equally, the value of the book won't be limited to people using the Morning Prayer Lectionary – it will be of use to many who never do, or who only want to use it on Sundays or as part of a non-Lectionary based pattern of prayer. Two possible patterns of reading the Psalms are suggested on pages 16–18.

Each reflection sits on a page with its corresponding Psalm refrain and prayer from the Common Worship Psalter.

Some of the longer psalms have been divided into shorter portions, each of which is given its own reflection (e.g. Psalm 18). The longest psalm, Psalm 119, is divided into eight parts, following the divisions found in *Common Worship Daily Prayer.*

The Psalms and the Bible

The book of the Psalms – sometimes also called the Psalter – has been at the centre of Jewish and Christian worship for over 2000 years, though individual psalms have been used in worship for much longer even than that. Indeed one of the most inspirational features of the Psalter is that it has been in constant use as a prayer book for at least 2000 years, if not longer. When we pray the words of the Psalms, we join our words to the words of those millions of Jews and Christians who have gone before us and have used this collection as their own prayer book.

Our English word 'psalm' comes from the Greek word *psalmos*, which means a song sung to harp music. Our name for the Psalms then seems to reflect how they were prayed. The Hebrew name for the Psalter is *Tehillim*, which means literally 'praises' and appears to be more connected to the content of the Psalms than to how they were prayed.

Five major types of psalms

The Hebrew name for the Psalter may have been 'praises', but you do not have to read very far through the Psalms to realize that not all psalms are psalms of praise. Some psalms contain far more grief and anger than they do praise. The further you read, the clearer it becomes that there are different types of psalms in the Psalter, and being able to recognize what type of psalm you are reading can be very helpful in understanding it better. There are five major types of psalms, although, of course, not all psalms fit easily into one category or another.

- **Hymns** – Many of the Psalms fall into the category of hymns. Hymns are focused around God, who he was and is, and what he has done. They often begin and end with a call to praise, with a middle section that describes more about who God is (as, for example, in Psalm 33).
- **Laments** – Another large group of psalms are best described as laments. Some laments are communal; others are individual. These psalms all have a similar form: they begin and end with a plea to God begging him to hear their cry, with a middle section that lays out the nature of the disaster. With the exception of Psalm 88, which is full of despair from beginning to end, the psalms of lament are striking in that they express their faith in God despite what is going on around them.

- **Thanksgiving psalms** – Connected to the laments are the thanksgiving psalms, which give thanks to God for what he has done to help the psalmist. They are most likely to have been used to accompany a sacrifice of thanksgiving in the temple.
- **Royal psalms** – The royal psalms are all, as their title suggests, about kings. They praise God for the king; they celebrate the king and all he has done; they pray for the king and declare his righteousness. Royal psalms are in form quite different from each other, and the only thing that connects them is their interest in the king.
- **Wisdom psalms** – The wisdom psalms stand out from the rest since they appear to arise less from immediate events of catastrophe or celebration and more from a particular way of looking at the world (a perspective that they share with books such as Proverbs and Ecclesiastes). As a result they focus attention on the importance of wisdom and the fear of the Lord, and seem to be instructing their hearers into a better way of being. A good example of a wisdom psalm is Psalm 1.

As well as these five major types of psalms there are a number of psalms that would best fit under the heading of **miscellaneous**. These psalms are quite different from each other and almost defy categorization.

Orientation, disorientation and reorientation

Scholars use the five major categories as a tool for understanding more about the Psalms and how they were first used. The Old Testament scholar and theologian Walter Brueggemann picked up this classification and took it a helpful step further as a means for us to read and understand the Psalms today. He observed that the majority of psalms in the categories above had one of three effects: orientation, disorientation and reorientation.

What he meant by this was that there are some psalms that reflect the ordinariness of life. These he identified as psalms of **orientation** (see for example Psalm 33). These psalms arise out of and speak into lives that are settled, clear and purposeful. In these God's presence is easily discerned and identified.

The problem is that our lives can all too easily fall apart – with very little notice. When they do, we feel as though we are sucked down into a deep pit and that God is absent and uncaring. Psalms of **disorientation** (such as Psalm 22) are written out of such an experience, but nevertheless are addressed to God and reflect the assurance of a relationship with God despite the events that crush us.

Psalms of **reorientation** (such as Psalm 103) reflect faith after catastrophe and explore the nature of faith in God following such an experience.

In other words, the majority of psalms speak out of and into genuine experience – experience that resonates as strongly today as it did when the Psalms were first written. Indeed, it is the genuineness of this experience that means that the Psalms still speak powerfully to so many people; they are not just of historic interest, but remain profoundly relevant as prayers that speak out of real emotion. Many people have found over the years that praying with the Psalms has helped them bring what they are feeling to God in both the good times and the bad.

The five books of the Psalter

So far we have looked at the groupings of individual psalms based on their form and content. It is worth noting, however, that the Psalter has already grouped the Psalms together in five collections (1–41; 42–72; 73–89; 90–106; 107–150). The collections are each marked at the end with a doxology or blessing (see 41.13; 72.18-19; 89.52), and the final book ends with a grand doxology of a whole psalm. It appears that these five collections had a life as collections before they were all gathered together into one book. This is because there are some duplicates (see, for example, Psalms 14 and 53). Every time there are duplicate psalms, they appear in two different collections. The best explanation for this is that by the time the Psalter was gathered together as a whole collection, the smaller collections were so well known as they were that it was not possible to take the duplicate psalms out.

Having said this, the whole Psalter itself has movement within it. Although lament and praise are woven together throughout the whole book, there are many more laments in the first half of the Psalter and many more thanksgivings in the second half, until you get to the end of the Psalter, which contains pure unadulterated praise. It is also worth noting that the central psalm (if you count volume of words not psalm numbers) is Psalm 88, which is the psalm mentioned above as being despairing from beginning to end. It is almost as though the whole Psalter sinks into deep disorientation at its heart before turning the corner into reorientation. As a result, the Psalter as a whole reflects the movement of many psalms of lament, which journey into the depths of despair and then out again in praise and thanksgiving.

Poetry and parallelism

Hebrew poetry, while recognizable as poetry, is quite different from English poetry, since rhythm and rhyme are less important for it than assonance and parallelism. Parallelism, in particular, is an unusual and striking feature of Hebrew poetry. In its basic form parallelism, as its name suggests, means that what has just been said is repeated in a slightly different form in the line below. See, for example, Psalm 24.1-2:

The earth is the Lord's and all that fills it,
the compass of the world and all who dwell therein.
For he has founded it upon the seas
and set it firm upon the rivers of the deep.

As this example illustrates, it is this parallelism that lends the psalms poetic rhythm, rather than the syllables of individual lines. Another key feature is that the parallel lines match each other in word order and structure. You can see this particularly clearly in the next verse of Psalm 24 (v.3):

'Who shall ascend the hill of the Lord,
or who can rise up in his holy place?'

The balancing of the question word in the two lines again lends a poetic rhythm to the text.

The parallelism is not, however, always **symmetrical**. Sometimes it contains opposites (and is therefore called **antithetical parallelism**). See for example, Psalm 18.27:

With the pure you show yourself pure,
but with the crooked you show yourself perverse.

Or it can develop an idea (called **step or synthetic parallelism**), as in Psalm 103.13:

As a father has compassion on his children,
so is the Lord merciful towards those who fear him.

As a result, one of the key features of Hebrew poetry is the way in which the form of the poem carries its content through repetition, contrast and development.

An extreme version of this is acrostic psalms, in which each paragraph, line or couplet begins with the next letter of the Hebrew alphabet. Examples of this can be found in Psalms 9, 10, 25, 34, 111, 112, 119 and 145. Unfortunately, as these are almost impossible to translate into English like this, we cannot normally see them. The most elaborate of these is Psalm 119, which begins each paragraph (of 8 lines each) with consecutive letters of the Hebrew alphabet.

A note on *Selah*: A little word that occurs 71 times in the Psalms is the word *selah* (see Psalm 3, for example) – it is there in most English translations too. Much has been written about this very small word, largely because it is hard to be sure what it means. Possibly the most likely explanation is that it indicated a break when the musicians played some music before the words of the psalm began again.

Titles and authorship

Many people want to discuss the authorship of the book of Psalms, but the problem is that it is very difficult to do so with any level of certainty. Most psalms have a title or ascription. Two thirds of these attribute the Psalms to David; the others are ascribed to a wide variety of other authors. There can be no doubt that some of the Psalms are very old indeed, but it is almost impossible to prove (or disprove) actual authorship. In reality, the authorship of the book of Psalms is of lesser importance than for other books. The Psalms have been prayed, prayed again and re-prayed for such a long time that who first said them has become less relevant than who is praying them again now. The Psalms have many, many authors – a new one each time they are prayed from the heart.

Paula Gooder

The Psalms in the life of the Church

'Let the word of Christ dwell in you richly; teach and admonish one another in all wisdom; and with gratitude in your hearts sing psalms, hymns and spiritual songs to God.' (Colossians 3.16)

Reading the book of Psalms is one of the very best ways of allowing the word of Christ to dwell in you and to dwell in the community of the Church.

The book of Psalms is the core of the prayer book of Jesus and his disciples. Jesus would have learned and prayed the psalms within the family, the synagogue and the temple. According to the gospels, Jesus applies words from the book of Psalms to his own ministry on numerous occasions: in answering temptation (Psalm 91.11-12 in Matthew 4.6 and Luke 4.10-11); in describing his teaching ministry (Psalm 78.2 in Matthew 13.35); on Palm Sunday (Psalm 118 in Matthew 21, Mark 12 and Luke 13); in demonstrating that he is the Lord's anointed (Psalm 110 in Matthew 22.44, Mark 12.36 and Luke 20.42) and, of course, from the cross (Psalm 22 in Matthew 27.46 and Mark 15.34).

For the early Church, the words of the psalms rapidly became words that shaped worship and prayer and through which the Church responded to the grace of God in Jesus Christ. Yet the Psalms were more than this: the Psalms were a place where the Church discovered and rediscovered Christ as Lord and King, as prophet and teacher, as servant and saviour.

Yet what place do the Psalms have in our own traditions of worship and prayer? The book of Psalms is often neglected in the normal Sunday worship of Anglican congregations. Psalms are rarely read as part of the Sunday lectionary or spoken or sung together by the community. For that reason they are rarely read privately either. Many Christians therefore lack a rich and textured knowledge of one of the greatest resource for prayer the world has ever known. There is undiscovered treasure here.

Reading the Psalms together

There is no single 'right' way to say or sing or explore the Psalms. The Church has evolved two main ways of using the Psalms in worship.

The first is to read (or chant) them 'in course' as part of the discipline of daily prayer, first in monastic communities and then as part of Morning and Evening Prayer in churches. In the *Book of Common*

Prayer lectionary, the whole Psalter is set to be read from beginning to end at Morning and Evening Prayer over the course of every month (see pages 16–17). In some other schemes, the psalms are distributed over the course of the week or the month, not in order from 1 to 150 but according to different themes, but the aim remains to read the whole Psalter.

The second way to read them is to choose particular psalms as vehicles for prayer and worship because of their theme or meaning at different times of the year. The psalms of praise have often been translated metrically as hymns. The psalms in the Sunday Eucharistic lectionary are chosen for their theme and relationship to the readings.

Psalms need to be read with understanding, especially when read in the whole congregation. Reading the Psalter in its course at Morning or Evening Prayer is more like reading the Old and New Testament aloud (except that the whole congregation shares in both reading and listening). We are not meant to put ourselves into the words quite as we do when singing a hymn or saying a prayer together. The normal pattern of reading in this way is antiphonal: different parts of the congregation say alternate verses or half verses with a pause at the colon to take in the parallelism in the poetry. We read to one another and reflect on what we read.

Reading or singing the psalms according to their theme is a different matter. Here we are using the psalms as vehicles for our praise or lament. We are meant to put ourselves into the words just as we would when singing a hymn. The normal method of reading in this way is either all together (congregational) or with a reader or cantor singing the words and everyone joining in a regular refrain (responsorial).

Reading the psalms privately as part of daily prayers is somewhere between the two. On some days, saying the psalm as part of the Daily Office can seem like an additional Bible reading: we are listening to the text more than praying it aloud. On other days, the psalm will put into words exactly what we want to say to God that day.

The vocabulary and grammar of prayer

The psalms form and shape our prayers in deep and significant ways. They provide a deep vocabulary and grammar for our prayers as we allow the word of God to dwell in our own lives and within our community in this way. We learn the vocabulary and grammar of praise: learning to rejoice in all circumstances; to set delight in God at the centre of our lives. We learn to praise God for his nature, for his actions, for his constancy, for his grace. Yet we learn as well that, in William Blake's words, joy and woea are woven fine. We discover how to cry out to God in our darkest times. We are taught how to pray in anguish, in doubt, in fear, in abandonment, in rage and in every kind of danger.

It is often hard to put both positive and negative emotion into words. The psalms offer us a vocabulary and grammar to bring the whole of our lives before God, the neat parts and the mess, our sin and our thankfulness, and make it somehow an offering of prayer. It is particularly important, in a lifetime of discipleship, to bring our struggles, our wrestling, our anguish to God and to be able to articulate anger, doubt and sometimes even hatred as part of seeing those emotions transfigured and transformed. The psalms have verses that are, by tradition, bracketed as not suitable for public worship but which nevertheless inform and shape our private prayers in those most challenging of times (see for example Psalm 137.7-9).

The Psalms as a whole offer us a quarry where we find over the course of a lifetime many rich and good things: phrases, verses, half verses that become food for meditation, that we set deep within our spiritual life like jewels, that become intrinsically part of who we are as followers of Jesus Christ. Part of praying the psalms is taking time to discover these channels of grace, to live within them and to allow them to dwell within us.

Christ the King

The Psalter has always been both an invitation to dwell on God's written word (caught by Psalm 1) and a witness to God's living Word, the Christ (caught by Psalm 2). As we have seen, many of the psalms were originally composed for use by God's anointed, the king. Psalms 2 and 110, and many others, speak directly of the king who will come, the Messiah, the Christ (Hebrew and Greek for anointed). To the Christian, therefore, the Psalter is more than a rich resource for prayer. It is also a handbook and guide for exploring the inexhaustible riches of Christ. Use it deeply and use it well.

Steven Croft

Psalm table for reading the Psalms over the course of a month (BCP)

In the *Book of Common Prayer* lectionary, the whole Psalter is set to be read from beginning to end at Morning and Evening Prayer over the course of every month, according to the following table.

Psalms 1–5	Day 1	Morning Prayer
Psalms 6–8	Day 1	Evening Prayer
Psalms 9–11	Day 2	Morning Prayer
Psalms 12–14	Day 2	Evening Prayer
Psalms 15–17	Day 3	Morning Prayer
Psalm 18	Day 3	Evening Prayer
Psalms 19–21	Day 4	Morning Prayer
Psalms 22–23	Day 4	Evening Prayer
Psalms 24–26	Day 5	Morning Prayer
Psalms 27–29	Day 5	Evening Prayer
Psalms 30–31	Day 6	Morning Prayer
Psalms 32–34	Day 6	Evening Prayer
Psalms 35–36	Day 7	Morning Prayer
Psalm 37	Day 7	Evening Prayer
Psalms 38–40	Day 8	Morning Prayer
Psalms 41–43	Day 8	Evening Prayer
Psalms 44–46	Day 9	Morning Prayer
Psalms 47–49	Day 9	Evening Prayer
Psalms 50–52	Day 10	Morning Prayer
Psalms 53–55	Day 10	Evening Prayer
Psalms 56–58	Day 11	Morning Prayer
Psalms 59–61	Day 11	Evening Prayer
Psalms 62–64	Day 12	Morning Prayer
Psalms 65–67	Day 12	Evening Prayer
Psalm 68	Day 13	Morning Prayer
Psalms 69–70	Day 13	Evening Prayer
Psalms 71–72	Day 14	Morning Prayer
Psalms 73–74	Day 14	Evening Prayer
Psalms 75–77	Day 15	Morning Prayer
Psalm 78	Day 15	Evening Prayer

Note: Where there are 31 days in the month, the Psalms for Day 30 are repeated.

Psalms 79–81	Day 16	Morning Prayer
Psalms 82–85	Day 16	Evening Prayer
Psalms 86–88	Day 17	Morning Prayer
Psalm 89	Day 17	Evening Prayer
Psalms 90–92	Day 18	Morning Prayer
Psalms 93–94	Day 18	Evening Prayer
Psalms 95–97	Day 19	Morning Prayer
Psalms 98–101	Day 19	Evening Prayer
Psalms 102–103	Day 20	Morning Prayer
Psalm 104	Day 20	Evening Prayer
Psalm 105	Day 21	Morning Prayer
Psalm 106	Day 21	Evening Prayer
Psalm 107	Day 22	Morning Prayer
Psalms 108–109	Day 22	Evening Prayer
Psalms 110–113	Day 23	Morning Prayer
Psalms 114–115	Day 23	Evening Prayer
Psalms 116–118	Day 24	Morning Prayer
Psalm 119.1-32	Day 24	Evening Prayer
Psalm 119.33-72	Day 25	Morning Prayer
Psalm 119.73-104	Day 25	Evening Prayer
Psalm 119.105-144	Day 26	Morning Prayer
Psalm 119.145-176	Day 26	Evening Prayer
Psalms 120–125	Day 27	Morning Prayer
Psalms 126–131	Day 27	Evening Prayer
Psalms 132–135	Day 28	Morning Prayer
Psalms 136–138	Day 28	Evening Prayer
Psalms 139–141	Day 29	Morning Prayer
Psalms 142–143	Day 29	Evening Prayer
Psalms 144–146	Day 30	Morning Prayer
Psalms 147–150	Day 30	Evening Prayer

Psalm table for Psalm 119 and the Psalms of Ascent

Common Worship provides two tables making use of Psalm 119 and the Psalms of Ascent (Psalms 121–131 and 133) on a weekly, fortnightly or monthly pattern.

Over a calendar month:

Day 1	119.1-8
Day 2	119.9-16
Day 3	119.17-24
Day 4	119.25-32
Day 5	119.33-40
Day 6	119.41-48
Day 7	119.49-56
Day 8	119.57-64
Day 9	119.65-72
Day 10	119.73-80
Day 11	119.81-88
Day 12	119.89-96
Day 13	119.97-104
Day 14	119.105-112
Day 15	119.113-120
Day 16	119.121-128
Day 17	119.129-136
Day 18	119.137-144
Day 19	119.145-152
Day 20	119.153-160
Day 21	119.161-168
Day 22	119.169-176
Day 23	121, 122
Day 24	123, 124
Day 25	125, 126
Day 26	127
Day 27	128
Day 28	129
Day 29	130
Day 30	131
Day 31	133

Over a week or fortnight:

Psalm 119 and the Psalms of Ascent may be used over a fortnight as follows:

Sunday	119.1-32
Monday	119.33-56
Tuesday	119.57-80
Wednesday	119.81-104
Thursday	119.105-128
Friday	119.129-152
Saturday	119.153-176

Sunday	121,122
Monday	123,124
Tuesday	125,126
Wednesday	127
Thursday	128
Friday	129,130
Saturday	131,133

Alternatively, Psalm 119 and the Psalms of Ascent may be used, together or alone, on a weekly cycle.

REFLECTIONS
ON THE
PSALMS

Psalm 1

**Blessed are they who have not walked
in the counsel of the wicked...**

'... planted by streams of water' (v.3)

The image, in Psalm 1, of trees planted by streams of water is a vibrant and evocative picture. It brings to mind refreshment and rootedness. The trees, which the psalmist invites us to imagine, are sustained not just occasionally but permanently from a source that invites them to sink their roots down deep and find nourishment and strength. Those who do not take the path of the wicked are like these trees, the psalmist tells us, with deep roots in the law of the Lord.

The wicked, in contrast, are not like sturdy trees but like chaff – dried out, lacking in substance and blown away by the breeze. Although we may not naturally make chaff the opposite of trees, it doesn't take much thought to see why the psalmist chose this particular contrast.

This opening psalm of the whole Psalter presents us, then, with two rich images that not only stir our imaginations but also present us with a choice. Will we choose to be like those who love God's law or those who spurn it? Will we, by the choice we make, find depth and refreshment, or aridity and flimsiness? By presenting us with this choice at the outset of the Psalter, Psalm 1 challenges us to choose what kind of life we will have and, as a result, how we will respond to the rest of the psalms that follow.

Reflection by **Paula Gooder**

PSALM 1

Refrain: *The Lord knows the way of the righteous.*

Prayer: *Christ our wisdom,
give us delight in your law,
that we may bear fruits of patience and peace
in the kingdom of the righteous;
for your mercy's sake.*

**Why are the nations in tumult,
and why do the peoples devise a vain plot?**

'Let us break their bonds asunder' (v.3)

Many people will hear the stern voice of the bass soloist in Handel's Messiah when reading this opening verse. 'Why do the nations so furiously rage together?' he sings. Pilgrims would gather in Jerusalem for the new-year festival and this psalm was spot on with its theme of the kingdom of God as a new king was crowned or an established king renewed in office.

So why do the nations still conspire and plot against the peaceful way of the Lord, or in the old words 'so furiously rage together'? Good question. The nations still believe what the rebellious choir in the *Messiah* sings, that they can burst asunder the bonds of the Lord and his anointed (v.3). We never learn. Even as I write this, there are over thirty wars still raging, often forgotten, in different parts of the globe.

There's a dark part of us that would still rather like an autocratic Lord to break the warlike nations with a rod of iron and dash them in pieces like a potter's vessel (v.9). Life would be so much simpler if the baddies were always baddies and the goodies were always like me. But the biblical story leads us to another kingdom where the King rules from a tree. He does indeed destroy evil but he does it only with the weapon of love.

Dare we follow this 'road less travelled' today?

Reflection by **John Pritchard**

Refrain: *The Lord is the strength of his people,
a safe refuge for his anointed.*

Prayer: *Most high and holy God,
lift our eyes to your Son
enthroned on Calvary;
and as we behold his meekness,
shatter our earthly pride;
for he is Lord for ever and ever.*

PSALM 2

Psalm 3

**Lord, how many are my adversaries;
many are they who rise up against me.**

'I lie down and sleep' (v.5)

Our imaginations are imprinted for life by the stories and pictures we were introduced to as children. The stories of Helen Bannerman about various children in India were stories I loved, and I cannot read this psalm without seeing the image of a little girl called Quasha (this was my favourite story because her name was like mine!) lying on her stomach under a tree in the jungle and reading aloud a new book she has bought, while more and more tigers gather around her. Eventually every tiger in the jungle is there. The tigers do not eat her up immediately because the story is so entertaining and they want to hear the end. She's oblivious to them.

Here, the hordes are encamped around the psalmist. There may be tens of thousands of them, but he is engrossed in something else: God. And absorbed in the worship of God, whom he recognizes as 'his glory', he is able to lie down and sleep. The difference between him and the little girl in the story is that he is not oblivious of anything; he is confident that he will ultimately be held even though his enemies set upon him. He is part of a bigger story than any their acts of violence can narrate. (The tigers discover something similar; they eventually set upon and destroy each other, but Quasha is saved by the book that rejoiced her heart.)

Reflection by **Ben Quash**

PSALM 3

Refrain: *You, Lord, are a shield about me.*

Prayer: *Shield us, Lord, from all evil,
and lift us from apathy and despair,
that even when we are terrified,
we may trust your power to save;
through Jesus Christ our Lord.*

**Answer me when I call, O God of my righteousness;
you set me at liberty when I was in trouble...**

'... it is you Lord, only' (v.8)

This evening psalm, often used in Night Prayer, gives us reassuring words to say as we entrust ourselves to sleep. It forms a pair with Psalm 3 and speaks of the betrayal and insult experienced by the psalmist and the foolishness of those who 'seek after falsehood' (v.2).

It fits David's time as a fugitive hounded by the 'nobles' who turned from him in favour of Saul. It chimes with the life of believers today as we see so much love of 'vain things' – an obsession with that which is empty – in our world. We are surrounded by false promises of satisfaction from sources that cannot deliver.

The test of faith comes when Saul seems to be winning, when sin seems to be paying, when emptiness seems to fill its supplicants with what they need – 'when their corn and wine and oil increase' (v.7). It is in those moments that we are called upon to exercise the strength of faith, believing that God can be trusted to 'lift up the light of [his] countenance upon us' (v.6).

The first dawn of God's light is gladness of heart (v.7), a deep inner joy that overrides outward difficulties. The fullness of God's light upon us and our world, though, is the promised shalom, the peace of God that penetrates every dimension of human life, putting right that which is wrong and proving that it is the Lord, only, who secures life for humanity.

Reflection by **Christopher Cocksworth**

Refrain: *In peace I will lie down and sleep.*

Prayer: *Give us today, O God,
a glad heart and a clear conscience,
that when we come to this day's end
we may rest in peace with Christ our Lord.*

Psalm 5

**Give ear to my words, O Lord;
consider my lamentation.**

'Lead me, Lord, in your righteousness' (v.8)

When Jesus calls his disciples he says 'Follow me'. In doing this he indicates that the life of faith is not static but dynamic; it involves walking in his footsteps. As Jesus' ministry unfolds, it becomes clear that the footsteps are leading somewhere. This is a journey to a destination, not an aimless ramble.

The way that we set out on this journey is therefore important. The psalmist's reference to the morning – the start of the day (v.3) – is significant here. We need to orient, and daily to re-orient, ourselves in God's direction, to align ourselves with his nature.

In this psalm we are offered a helpful model of how to do this. First, we can call out to God (v.1). This very act expresses the belief, made explicit in verse 4, that this is the sort of divine being on whom it is worth calling, because he orders the universe with justice. Second, we can draw physically or metaphorically close to God in worship (v.7). We may not always feel like it; indeed we may feel that God is far off. Nevertheless, we can make an active decision to set our compass Godwards (the Hebrew of verse 7 indicates a wilful intentional act), trying to discern the right way to live and then taking the first few halting steps along the path. This is what the Bible means by 'faith'. Here we can be greatly encouraged by joining with others (vv.12-14), for when his people gather God is in their midst to bless (Jeremiah 14.9).

Reflection by **Joanna Collicutt**

PSALM 5

Refrain: You, O Lord, will bless the righteous.

Prayer: Lord, protect us from the deceit
of flattering tongues and lying lips;
give us words of life which speak your truth
and bless your name;
through Jesus Christ our Lord.

**O Lord, rebuke me not in your wrath;
neither chasten me in your fierce anger.**

'Have mercy on me, Lord, for I am weak' (v.2)

To read this psalm is to go against the flow of our culture. These days we are continually pressed to boast of how well we are, how well we cope, how fit, how rejuvenated, how much improved by our current diet or exercise regime. We are even tempted to tweak our Facebook pics to prove it. The psalmist does just the opposite. He is frank about the fact that he is not a 'well' man. Indeed the confession 'I am weak' is followed by: I am 'weary ... wasted ... worn away' (vv.6,7). In some ways it's a relief to be able to say that, to be licensed by our liturgy to make that confession, and to make it in good company. For if the psalmist suffers and feels cut off and rebuked at the opening of the psalm, by verse 8 he knows that in spite of his weakness, he has got through to God. If he has, then so have I, who take his words on my lips and make them mine.

And what of these enemies, put to shame and confusion? Whoever his enemies were, ours are just those voices in our culture that want to shame us with our weakness, that only credit the young, the fit and the strong. Here God rebukes those voices and turns them back, so that we need never feel ashamed of our weakness with him, but rather bring it swiftly and simply to his mercy.

Reflection by **Malcolm Guite**

Refrain: Turn again, O Lord, and deliver my soul.

Prayer: Lord Jesus Christ,
may the tears shed in your earthly life
be balm for all who weep,
and may the prayers of your pilgrimage
give strength to all who suffer;
for your mercy's sake.

Psalm 7

**O Lord my God, in you I take refuge;
save me from all who pursue me, and deliver me.**

'I will give thanks' (v.17)

As in so many of the psalms, God is here described as a safe haven
to whom we can run in times of stress or danger – a refuge (v.1) and
a shield (v.10). Running to God in times of trouble is an expression
of faith. Yet in this case the psalmist's troubles seem to have arisen
from his attempt to walk God's way. He knows that God is just
(v.11), yet his current situation is marked by injustice and unmerited
persecution.

How is he to make sense of this? How are we to make sense of the
injustice that afflicts the whole world, and that sometimes touches
our nearest and dearest? The psalmist begins by exhorting God to
act in accordance with his nature. Even in the midst of his distressing
and confusing situation, he asserts that God is a God of justice.

Then somehow he seems to see the world differently. He observes a
kind of natural justice at work in the lives of those who do wrong;
their evil deeds and intentions ultimately rebound on them. In this
light he is able to do more than simply assert that God is good; he is
able to give thanks (v.17). From his dark situation has emerged the
virtue of gratitude. This is a virtue that begins with choosing to see
a situation as a gift, and that then has a knock-on effect on how we
act and feel: the ability to make music (v.17) is a sign that the dark
mood is lifting.

Reflection by **Joanna Collicutt**

PSALM 7

Refrain:	*Give judgement for me
according to my righteousness, O Lord.*

Prayer:	*Lord, your justice turns evil on itself:
move us to examine our hearts
and repent of all duplicity;
for the sake of Jesus Christ,
our Judge and righteous Saviour.*

O Lord our governor,
how glorious is your name in all the world!

'... praised out of the mouths of babes' (v.2)

Astronomy was a brand new science when this psalm was written. In Babylon, astronomers were beginning to map the sky, and they already had tables accurately predicting lunar eclipses. However, they had no concept whatever of the vast numbers and distances that we know are involved, now that present-day astronomers can turn their gamma-ray telescopes toward the void. To the believer, then as now, gazing upward results in awe at the majesty of God and his love for humanity (vv.4-5). To the sceptic, it affirms the impossibility of a Creator being responsible for such an insignificant thing as human life on planet Earth.

However, regardless of whether the scale of the cosmos strengthens a belief in God or does the opposite, there is someone whose thoughts are even more powerful than a psalmist or a scientist. That is a baby. A baby doesn't attempt to explain God, nor measure him, nor reject him. A baby just wonders (v.2).

Nobody – not even the world's most aggressive atheist – would tell an infant that it's ridiculous to be in awe of what is just a random evolutionary blip in the great godless progress of the cosmos. Instead, a child is encouraged to marvel.

Baby one; atheist nil.

Psalm 8 is a reminder that a little more childish astonishment would be good for us all from time to time.

Reflection by Peter Graystone

Refrain: *O Lord our governor,*
how glorious is your name in all the world!

Prayer: *We bless you, master of the heavens,*
for the wonderful order which enfolds this world;
grant that your whole creation
may find fulfilment in the Son of Man,
Jesus Christ our Saviour.

PSALM 8

Psalm 9

I will give thanks to you, Lord, with my whole heart;
I will tell of all your marvellous works.

'... let not mortals have the upper hand' (v.19)

All is well, it seems at first. The psalmist's enemies have been defeated. The wicked have been destroyed. God is to be praised, his miraculous deeds recalled and recounted.

But then the tone changes. 'Have mercy on me,' the psalmist pleads. What we have read so far has been more a statement of faith than an account of experience. It has told us what ought to be true.

Believing in God while living in God's world can be a frustrating experience. There is too much that is wrong with the world. It gives unbelievers a rod to beat us with. If there is a god, why does he not sort the world out? In particular, why do good people suffer and the wicked get away with it? And why does this happen on a global as well as an individual scale? There are too many dictatorships, too many places where people live in unnecessary poverty, too many of our sisters and brothers displaced from their homes and living in fear.

When we do not know how to pray for them, the psalmist's prayer can be ours too: 'let not mortals have the upper hand' (v.19). Despite all evidence to the contrary, God is indeed the one who will rule the world with righteousness and govern the peoples with equity. In the final contest between God and mortals, there can be only one winner.

Reflection by **Gillian Cooper**

Refrain: *You, Lord, have never failed those who seek you.*

Prayer: *Remember, Lord, all who cry to you*
from death's dark gates;
do not forget those whom the world forgets,
but raise your faithful ones to Zion's gate,
with your all-conquering Son,
Jesus Christ our Lord.

Why stand so far off, O Lord?
Why hide yourself in time of trouble?

'... forget not the poor' (v.12)

There are two questions posed in this psalm. We know the answer to one; we don't know the answer to the other.

The question to which we have an answer is: how do people get away with exploiting those who are poor? (v.2). It happens because the rules for trade between rich countries and poor countries have largely been set by the rich ones, who have most of the power. It's sobering to realize that the psalmist describes us who benefit from the unjust ways of the world's economics as 'wicked'. But it only requires one glance at the adverts that drive our media to confirm that we are people inclined to 'boast of [our] heart's desire' (v.3).

The question to which we don't have an answer is: why doesn't God intervene to stop injustice? (v.1). The writers of the Bible wrestled with this as much as we do. The psalm doesn't give an explanation, but it does show us how to pray on behalf of the world's poorest people. We start by acknowledging that we need God, because he is able to do things we cannot ('Arise O Lord God', v.12). We ask God to take the world's 'trouble and misery' into his hands, knowing that this is something he longs to do (v.14). And we pray in confidence that the final destiny of creation is for God to take control and restore justice 'for ever and ever' (v.17).

Reflection by **Peter Graystone**

Refrain: *You, Lord, have never failed those who seek you.*

Prayer: *When wickedness triumphs*
and the poor are betrayed,
come to your kingdom, strong and holy God,
destroy the masks of evil
and reign in our broken hearts;
through Jesus Christ our Lord.

PSALM 10

Psalm 11

In the Lord have I taken refuge;
how then can you say to me
'Flee like a bird to the hills ...'

'The Lord tries the righteous as well as the wicked' (v.6)

What a mess the world is in! Day after day brings news of violence. We live among people whose morals are appalling. People commit crimes and get away with it. How on earth can those of us who want to follow the Lord survive it? This psalm hints at three possibilities.

We could create a pure Christian community. We would cut ourselves off from encountering anyone who doesn't share our faith. We would read nothing but the Bible, watch nothing but *Songs of Praise*, and abandon the godless internet altogether. It is the equivalent of attempting to 'flee like a bird to the hills' (v.1).

Or we could confront power with power. It would mean arming ourselves for war. We would take on tyrants and vanquish them in the name of the God we worship, getting rid of the evil they inflict once and for all. It is our equivalent of bending the bows and fitting the arrows (v.2). Both of these approaches have been tried over the course of Christian history.

Alternatively, we can take refuge in God. It would involve trusting that the Lord knows what he is doing, and is ultimately God of 'the righteous as well as the wicked' (v.6). It means we would need to engage fully with the mess of the world, but seek to do the 'righteous deeds' that God loves (v.8). This is the one the psalmist urges us to choose.

Reflection by **Peter Graystone**

PSALM 11

Refrain: *The Lord's throne is in heaven.*

Prayer: *God of heaven,*
when the foundations are shaken
and there is no escape,
test us, but not to destruction,
look on the face of your anointed
and heal us in Jesus Christ your Son.

Help me, Lord, for no one godly is left;
the faithful have vanished from the whole human race.

'Like silver refined in the furnace' (v.6)

The mood of this psalm is one of intense isolation and alienation. The way of God is seen to be the way of truth; the light of God shows things up for what they are. Yet this truth is so often distorted or masked, especially by persuasive rhetoric, or telling people what they want to hear (vv.2,4).

Again and again in the Old Testament the true prophets are presented as people who name things that nobody wants to acknowledge (see, for example, 1 Kings 22). In a similar way, the New Testament writers warn repeatedly against the power of empty rhetoric (Matthew 6.7; 1 Corinthians 2.1-5) and slanderous words (2 Corinthians 12.20; Ephesians 4.31; Colossians 3.8; James 3.1-8).

Yet, says the psalmist, God's words are precious, purified in the fire (v.6) so that they illuminate with truth. In this he is prescient, for ultimately the eternal Word would come into the world as the light that shines in the darkness (John 1.1,5).

And what is the nature of its illumination? It throws things into a different sort of relief, and reveals what is wrong. This turns out to be the oppression and exploitation of those at the bottom of the pile (v.5), whose groans and calls for help are in danger of being drowned out by more comfortable cultural narratives. If we are to live in this light, we must trust God to watch over us (v.7) and then we must speak out in his name.

Reflection by **Joanna Collicutt**

Refrain: *You, O Lord, will watch over us.*

Prayer: *Lord, when faith is faint*
and speech veils our intentions,
restore us by your word of power and purity,
both now and for ever.

PSALM 12

Psalm 13

How long will you forget me, O Lord; for ever?
How long will you hide your face from me?

'Look upon me and answer' (v.3)

At its best, the Church is a school for relating. The life of faith teaches us to relate more deeply to God, other people and ourselves. This short psalm, maybe written on a sick bed, begins with the psalmist intensely focused on himself. The opening fourfold question of lament – 'How long...?' – reveals the anguish being felt within his heart. A reference to others follows, but they are seen as enemies and only looking on the psalmist's vulnerability with a sense of victory and pride. Both the relationship to his neighbours and to the psalmist's own self are in paralysis. Infused with anguish, the first four verses of this psalm are a statement of impatient hope. The author uses three urgent verbs to God: 'Look ... answer ... lighten' (v.3), calling on God to break in on his life.

What occurs in the psalmist's life between writing verse 4 and verse 5 we will never know, but it is transformative and decisive. The tone of the psalm shifts from one of impatience to trust, with talk of 'salvation' (v.5) and the ability to 'sing to the Lord' (v.6).

The last line of the psalm that declares that God 'has dealt so bountifully with me' resonates with those of us who have to look back in our lives, rather than dig around in the distracted and heated present, to read the love between its lines.

Reflection by **Mark Oakley**

Refrain: I love the Lord, for he has heard the voice
of my supplication.

Prayer: Jesus Christ, Son of God,
who passed through the dark sleep of death,
remember those who cry to you
in shame and silence and defeat
and raise them to your risen life,
for you are alive and reign for ever.

**The fool has said in his heart, 'There is no God.'
Corrupt are they, and abominable in their wickedness.**

'God is in the company of the righteous' (v.5)

This psalm is not concerned with the theoretical atheism that challenges faith today but with the practical outcomes of living as though God did not exist. The psalmist laments the way in which the world seems entirely to be run on human selfishness and self-centredness. As he sees it, there is no one who does good, and he grieves at the cost of wickedness, a cost that is borne chiefly, as it so often is, by the poor (vv.4,6).

But along with mourning comes judgement. The selfishness of the wicked reflects a fundamental lack of wisdom. Those judged corrupt fail to recognize that, from a heavenly perspective, all the children of earth are made to be responsible for one another. Those who reject this heavenly wisdom create a sterile and joyless world.

Yet God does not give up on the world of his creation. He is present in the company of the few who do act justly and he continues to protect the helpless. In small ways his people still bear witness to the joyful promise that God holds out to humanity, a promise that will come from Zion. From a Christian viewpoint, this is a prophecy that looks towards the age of the Messiah, the coming of the king of righteousness and peace. For us, it means that our small daily efforts to live fairly and responsibly are infinitely worthwhile.

Reflection by **Angela Tilby**

Refrain: *The fear of the Lord is the beginning of wisdom.*

Prayer: *God of heaven,*
look with mercy on all who are consumed
by ignorance and greed,
and let the children of earth know
that you are God for ever.

PSALM 14

Psalm 15

Lord, who may dwell in your tabernacle?
Who may rest upon your holy hill?

'Whoever leads an uncorrupt life ...' (v.2)

But who is that? Which of us can guarantee our entitlement to a place atop this holy hill? Which of us can make our feet firm against the chaos not only of life but of the human heart, with all its distractions and mixed motives? We remember the sense of extraordinary unworthiness Simon Peter feels in Luke 5 as he is confronted, and his ship is destabilized, by the vast number of fish that suddenly fill his nets. He found his life secured for him, but knew he could not possibly have earned this new standing with his Lord in the face of the world's threats.

The Christian belief, though, is that he did not need to earn it. That's what the Book of Common Prayer means when in the baptismal service it asks God's mercy to 'grant to this child that thing which *by nature she cannot have*'. By grace we take our place on the hill of the Lord, which for Christians is to say that by grace we are 'incorporated into Christ', who alone is uncorrupt. Then, where Christ goes, we go, and where Christ enters in, we enter in.

The incorporation of Christians into Christ – our sharing with him in name, and in all the benefits of his death and resurrection – means that when the gates of the city on the hill are thrown open, and the King of glory comes in, we come in too. It is a triumphal entry made possible by the free and gracious work of God.

Reflection by **Ben Quash**

Refrain: Through the greatness of your mercy,
I will come into your house.

Prayer: Lord, lead us to our heavenly home
by single steps of self-restraint
and deeds of righteousness;
through the grace of Jesus Christ our Lord.

**Preserve me, O God, for in you have I taken refuge;
I have said to the Lord, 'You are my lord...'**

'In the night watches he instructs my heart' (v.6)

It can be lonely in the night watches. That is the time when the mind starts to list all the things that should have been done but have not. It is the time when problems churn around the head. You put the light on, make a list, try to get back to sleep, get up, make a cup of tea ...

It seems the psalmist has an even bigger worry. We know the human fate is to die. But will that be the end of us? Will we simply disappear into nothingness, the 'Pit' of Old Testament thinking? In the dark of the night, our worst fears emerge. Are we putting our trust in the wrong place? The psalmist sees the attractions of 'idols', other objects of worship, but turns away from them. Our deepest fears can be faced only with the aid of God himself: 'in the night watches he instructs my heart' (v.6).

So what does the heart then know? That God is there for those who seek refuge in him. That we have a 'goodly heritage', the long story of our faith, the example of those who have gone before us. That in God may be found life and joy, which never fails for all eternity. When we are most afraid, the psalmist gives us the words to express our trust in this God, the only power in the universe that can save us.

Reflection by **Gillian Cooper**

Refrain: *The Lord is at my right hand; I shall not fall.*

Prayer: *Give to us, Lord Christ,
the fullness of grace,
your presence and your very self,
for you are our portion and our delight,
now and for ever.*

PSALM 16

Psalm 17

**Hear my just cause, O Lord; consider my complaint;
listen to my prayer, which comes not from lying lips.**

'Hide me under the shadow of your wings' (v.8)

The psalmist is under siege here and convinced of his own righteousness. Do we perhaps feel a little uncomfortable with the author's conviction that he is unquestionably in the right? If we do, it may be because his experience finds some resonance with our own. Like the author, we long for justice in the world. We, too, struggle when the 'unrighteous' appear to prosper, their greed and wickedness seeming to go unpunished. We, too, may be tempted to thank God that we 'are not like other people' (Luke 18.11), seeing ourselves as 'righteous' in comparison. Where, on such occasions, do we take our pride, our anger and our fear?

Despite his inner turmoil, the psalmist here continues to reach out to God in hope and trust (v.8). Other psalms use the image of the shadow of God's wings as both a place of safety (Psalms 57.2; 91.4) and of rejoicing (Psalm 63.8). There is an ancient Celtic morning prayer that uses the same imagery when seeking God's protective power: 'Even as I clothe my body... Cover Thou my soul with the shadow of Thy wing' (*Carmina Gadelica*).

We need to learn – and learn again – that whatever turbulence we encounter in our lives, it is only by the side of our heavenly Father – 'under the shadow of [God's] wings' – that we can know sanctuary and peace.

Reflection by **Barbara Mosse**

Refrain: *Deliver me, O Lord, by your hand.*

Prayer: *Generous Lord,*
deliver us from
all envious thoughts,
    and when we are tempted by the desire for wealth,
    let us see your face;
    for your abundance is enough to clothe our lack;
    through Jesus Christ our Lord.

**I love you, O Lord my strength.
The Lord is my crag, my fortress and my deliverer...**

'... my rock ... my shield, the horn of my salvation' (v.2)

If you chose nine names for God today, what would they be?

Psalm 18 begins with a short direct song of devotion to God who is given nine deeply personal descriptions (my crag, my fortress, my shield ...).

These two verses are the prelude to the longest psalm of testimony and thanksgiving in the Psalter. Psalm 18 is closely linked to the life of David the King, not only by the heading and the final verse, but also by its setting in 2 Samuel 22, at the end of the stories of David.

This prelude gives way to four graphic verses that describe the danger faced by the psalmist and his cry for help. But these prepare the way for the even more graphic, powerful description of the Lord coming to the rescue of his chosen anointed. Here is earthquake, wind and fire in abundance – in the words of Robert Grant's hymn 'O worship the King': 'His chariots of wrath the deep thunderclouds form, And dark is his path on the wings of the storm'.

God is in heaven and the psalmist on earth. Yet prayer is a powerful bridge between the two. The Lord hears the psalmist's cry of help. He parts the heavens and comes down. The first act of salvation is the Lord's appearing.

If you chose nine names for God today, based on your life story, what would they be?

Reflection by **Steven Croft**

Refrain: *The Lord my God shall make my darkness
     to be bright.*

Prayer: *From your royal throne, O God,
     you sent your living Word
     to pierce the gloom of oppression;
     so, in our souls' night,
     come with your saving help
     and penetrate our darkness with the rays of your glory
     in Jesus Christ our Lord.*

PSALM 18

Psalm 18, vv.17-30

He reached down from on high and took me;
he drew me out of the mighty waters.

'You also shall light my candle' (v.29)

The great crescendo of the Lord appearing is followed by a more gentle song of praise. The psalmist describes his own salvation. God rescues him from danger and death, and restores him to liberty and life.

There are at least three ways to read the middle section of Psalm 18. We read the psalm as the testimony of David and the later kings, giving thanks for the deliverance from enemies in battle. The moral framework fits the book of Deuteronomy and history as told by the books of Samuel and Kings: God rescues only those who lead good lives.

As Christians, we read the psalm as the testimony of God's anointed, the Christ, who brings God's kingdom in his own death and resurrection. God has delivered his Son from the deep waters of death. God's own son is without sin.

But as Christians we also read the psalm, by faith, as a testimony of God's own grace in our lives. For we have experienced God's salvation: God has parted the heavens and come down and drawn us out of the mighty waters, not because of our own goodness but because of the goodness and sacrifice of Christ.

Because of his goodness and his salvation, we pray in faith: 'the Lord my God shall make my darkness to be bright' (v.29).

Reflection by **Steven Croft**

PSALM 18

Refrain: *The Lord my God shall make my darkness*
to be bright.

Prayer: *From your royal throne, O God,*
you sent your living Word
to pierce the gloom of oppression;
so, in our souls' night,
come with your saving help
and penetrate our darkness with the rays of your glory
in Jesus Christ our Lord.

As for God, his way is perfect;
the word of the Lord is tried in the fire.

'He makes my feet like hinds' feet' (v.34)

Where will you find the strength you need for this day, this week and this year? Where will you find the courage to live well as a disciple, to attempt great things for God, to fight the good fight, to overcome the challenges you face? Too many Christians live defeated lives.

The whole purpose of Psalm 18 is to impart resilience and strength in our discipleship. The psalm rehearses in public worship and in private prayer God's power, majesty and might. We recall everything that God has done for us in Christ and in the story of our lives.

As we remember together, so we find the courage and strength we need to face the challenges and trials this day and this season bring. We draw down into the present the memories and lessons of the past. Prayer is not a retreat into safety and security for its own sake; prayer is a daily retreat in order to find fresh strength, inner courage and new resources for the battle ahead.

Sometimes that confidence will overflow in the kind of joy that leads us to attempt extraordinary things for God: treading on the heights and leaping over walls. Sometimes there will simply be a fresh determination: enough grace for this day to live faithfully and well in the face of adversity and evil. Both kinds of strength are found in abundance in thanksgiving and in praise.

Reflection by **Steven Croft**

Refrain: *The Lord my God shall make my darkness*
to be bright.

Prayer: *From your royal throne, O God,*
you sent your living Word
to pierce the gloom of oppression;
so, in our souls' night,
come with your saving help
and penetrate our darkness with the rays of your glory
in Jesus Christ our Lord.

PSALM 18

Psalm 19

**The heavens are telling the glory of God
and the firmament proclaims his handiwork.**

'Their sound has gone out into all lands' (v.4)

This is a wonderful psalm that moves seamlessly from an ecstatic delight in God's creation to praise for his all-encompassing law. Then, at the end, it embarks on a personal and moving plea for integrity that comes from the depths of the human heart. The cosmos, the law and the heart are not only perfectly made by God but also intimately connected. God's handiwork is a unity, which we are called to participate in as well as to enjoy. The strength and purity of the sun is the visible sign of God's wisdom holding all things together, just as the universality of the Torah gives guidance for the whole of life.

Given that the psalm brings together the cosmic and the human it is not surprising that the early Christians saw in its imagery a metaphor for the incarnation. The picture of the sun as a giant rising in the east and sinking in the west spoke to them of Christ running the whole course of human life as our champion and shedding his light and grace on the whole world.

This is a psalm to arouse our spiritual imaginations, to extend our sense of wonder at the natural world and to draw us into a deeper love for the law of God inscribed in our hearts.

Reflection by **Angela Tilby**

PSALM 19

Refrain: *The commandment of the Lord is pure
and gives light to the eyes*

Prayer: *Christ, the sun of righteousness,
rise in our hearts this day,
enfold us in the brightness of your love
and bear us at the last to heaven's horizon;
for your love's sake.*

**May the Lord hear you in the day of trouble,
the name of the God of Jacob defend you.**

'We will call only on the name of the Lord our God' (v.7)

When we first fall in love, the name of the one we love is sheer magic. It glows whenever we hear it. To say to someone, 'I love you, thingummybob,' isn't very convincing. Names are deeply significant. To use someone's name is to value them and give them their full identity. So too 'the name of the Lord' was supremely significant for God's people. They would praise his name and call upon his name and trust his name. They believed that the name of the God of Jacob would protect them (v.1), and while some took pride in chariots and some in horses (the usual signs of strength), their pride was in the name of the Lord their God (v.7).

It pays not to forget names. And for Christians the name above all names is that of Jesus, because it's that name that has come to sum up all our hope in the grace of God and the gift of new life. It was when I finally twigged about the centrality of Jesus that my own faith suddenly made sense. It's no surprise that the Jesus Prayer has become so significant in the West as well as in Orthodox churches; it names Jesus, continually. 'Lord Jesus Christ, Son of God, have mercy on me, a sinner.'

May the name of Jesus be close to our heart this day.

Reflection by **John Pritchard**

Refrain: We will call on the name of the Lord our God.

Prayer: Merciful God,
purify our hearts in the flame of your Spirit
and transform our toil into an offering of praise,
that we may reject the proud rule of might
and trust in Christ alone,
for he is our Lord for ever and ever.

PSALM 20

41

Psalm 21

**The king shall rejoice in your strength, O Lord;
how greatly shall he rejoice in your salvation!**

'He asked of you life and you gave it him' (v.4)

One of the enduring images from the coronation of Elizabeth II is of the young queen entering Westminster Abbey to the sounds of Handel's *Zadok the Priest*. The rhythmic and melodic build-up is long, the crescendo is gradual and relentless – almost unbearable – until the singers burst out of the musical texture accompanied by drums and brass to announce the new monarch.

This psalm is often categorized by scholars as one of the royal psalms, and, within that category, as a psalm possibly sung at a coronation or at the anniversary of a coronation. It is a psalm designed to stir the hearts of all who would defend God's people against their enemies. It may have been sung before a battle, as a way of boosting morale and confidence, perhaps like Henry V's speech in which Shakespeare has him rallying his troops, outnumbered and facing death as they are, ready to die for their country.

As a system of government, monarchy has its detractors, but the figure of the monarch in the Hebrew Scriptures is very clear: kings are there primarily to defend and protect, to defend their people from their enemies, and also to defend the poor (in Hebrew *anawim*) from persecution. Kings are especially responsible and accountable for creating a just society for aliens, widows and orphans. In this psalm it is clear that this human authority derives its authenticity (v.7) from trusting solely in God.

Reflection by **Lucy Winkett**

PSALM 21

Refrain: *The king puts his trust in the Lord.*

Prayer: *Crown us, O God, but with humility,
and robe us with compassion,
that, as you call us into the kingdom of your Son,
we may strive to overcome all evil
by the power of good
and so walk gently on the earth
with you, our God, for ever.*

**My God, my God, why have you forsaken me,
and are so far from my salvation,
from the words of my distress?**

'You have answered me!' (v.21)

Christian readers of Psalm 22 struggle to hear its opening verse without the dreadful echo of Jesus' cry from the cross also ringing in their ears: 'My God, my God why have you forsaken me?' It is a cry laden with desolation and hopelessness and one that many of us will relate to at the very worst times in our lives.

It is important, though, as we read this psalm not to stop at verse 1. The opening verse begins with despair and bleakness, but the psalm does not remain there. One of its keys features is that it goes on to look backwards at all God has done in the past ('On you was I cast ever since I was born; you are my God even from my mother's womb', v.10) and forwards to all God will do in the future ('The poor shall eat and be satisfied; those who seek the Lord shall praise him', v.26).

When we are sucked down into the pits of misery, we can feel profoundly cut off not just from friends, family and God but also from happier times in our lives. Psalm 22 reminds us powerfully that, no matter how we might feel, the God who has always loved us never changes. This God has always loved us and will never stop. Even when we are sucked down into the darkest pit of despair God is there with us.

Reflection by **Paula Gooder**

Refrain: *Be not far from me, O Lord.*

Prayer: *Restless with grief and fear,
the abandoned turn to you:
in every hour of trial,
good Lord, deliver us,
O God most holy, God most strong,
whose wisdom is the cross of Christ.*

PSALM 22

Psalm 23

**The Lord is my shepherd;
therefore can I lack nothing.**

'... and my cup shall be full' (v.5)

Running on empty? The pastoral setting for Psalm 23 with its metaphor of shepherd and sheep can sometimes belie its strength, and there's a poetic softness to the text – all 'green pastures' and 'still waters' – which may lull us into imagining it to be a gentle, even innocuous thing. But this is a strong psalm for lean times.

The psalm takes seriously the reality that life is often demanding. Wilderness and shadow, valley and trouble are common human experiences faced by us all. But the psalm also suggests that this harsh reality is, in God's care, neither the only truth nor the last word. Wanderings through a confusing landscape may turn out to be journeys on guided pathways. The agitation of shadows may lead into stillness. The dark valley may in time reveal itself to be a place of restoration.

These contrasting possibilities culminate in the line 'and my cup shall be full' (v.5). How welcome is this revelation. So many of our actions (and inactions) emerge from a sense (or fear) of emptiness, of lack, of waste and of loss. But in the presence of the shepherd, all will be full.

So what might become possible in and around us if we recognize this moment, this day or this season as being one of fullness, a gift from God, containing all that we need to thrive and to bring our goodness to the world?

Reflection by **Ian Adams**

PSALM 23

Refrain: *I will dwell in the house of the Lord for ever.*

Prayer: *O God, our sovereign and shepherd,
who brought again your Son Jesus Christ
from the valley of death,
comfort us with your protecting presence
and your angels of goodness and love,
that we also may come home
and dwell with him in your house for ever.*

**The earth is the Lord's and all that fills it,
the compass of the world and all who dwell therein.**

'... the King of glory shall come in' (v.7)

This is one of the great psalms of movement. It is not difficult to imagine bands of pilgrims chanting its words as they climb the hill towards the city of Jerusalem. Indeed, I found myself doing the same when I entered Jerusalem for the first time. But the movement it describes is deeper and fuller than even the holy city can absorb.

The psalm defines the origin of the world in the movement of God's will. 'The earth is Lord's' (v.1) and everything that fills it because God is the creator of all things.

The God who so carefully creates, calls humanity to rise to its full dignity and move up into the presence of God. Like Jacob we are to dream of God, to desire God, to seek the face of God and to yearn for the blessing of God.

Unlike Jacob, we are to be without guile, neither swearing an oath to a lie nor lifting up our souls to falsehood (see Genesis 27.18-24). So how, when God comes to the world as 'the King of glory', can our heads be lifted up? How dare we even touch, let alone open, the everlasting doors that give God entry? Will not our eyes be blinded by such glorious light?

No, because God moves to the earth in the glory of Jesus Christ in whom humanity is re-founded and the world is re-set by the glory of God's grace.

Reflection by **Christopher Cocksworth**

Refrain: *The Lord of hosts: he is the King of glory.*

Prayer: *O Lord of hosts,*
purify our hearts
that the King of glory may come in,
your Son, Jesus our redeemer.

PSALM 24

Psalm 25

To you, O Lord, I lift up my soul;
O my God, in you I trust.

'The hidden purpose of the Lord is for those who fear him
and he will show them his covenant.' (v.13)

Can God make a bowl of porridge that is too big for God to eat? Can God make a weight that God cannot lift? If you have ever tried to solve these riddles, then you'll know these questions can't be answered – at least adequately. But philosophers and theologians down the ages have always said that if we try and trap God in our own reasoning, and frame him in our own language, we'll always miss the point. God is beyond our rationality. Placing God in the midst of a logical contradiction doesn't do anything to God. Except perhaps amuse him.

Many of our best-loved psalms don't emerge out of philosophical speculations. Instead, they arise out of anxiety, crises and pain. The psalmist here fears abandonment – one of our deepest human fears. Alone, we are afraid. The psalmist also fears that the Israelites have brought this on themselves, through the shame of their action. God is implored for mercy and begged for grace. Will God turn his eyes and his face to the writer once more?

Yet the psalmist can be at peace. God is not only Lord, but a true friend. The mystics say that if God has one weakness, it is his heart. It is too soft. God cannot fail to love us. He does not know how to forget us. God cannot abandon his people. So we can take refuge in the God who chooses to abide with his people and love them. Yes, *chooses* to abide. There is no place that God would rather be than with us. He abides with us. God is Emmanuel.

Reflection by **Martyn Percy**

PSALM 25

Refrain: Remember, Lord, your compassion and love.

Prayer: Free us, God of mercy,
from all that keeps us from you;
relieve the misery of the anxious and the ashamed
and fill us with the hope of peace;
through Jesus Christ our Lord.

Give judgement for me, O Lord,
for I have walked with integrity.

'For your love is before my eyes' (v.3)

We set out on the way of God by orienting ourselves Godwards and aligning ourselves with his nature (see Psalm 5, p.22), but his way can be hard, and it can be all too easy to wander away from it. One approach to this challenge is to think of life in terms of two very different ways. For example, the Sermon on the Mount contrasts the narrow gate and hard road that leads to life with the wide gate and easy road that leads to destruction (Matthew 7.13-14). So, we might think it advisable to learn the marks of the wrong way, to recognize the sort of folk who walk it, and then steer clear of it.

This approach is often to be found in the psalms. Indeed the Psalter opens with the statement 'Blessed are they who have not walked in the counsel of the wicked' (Psalm 1.1). Psalm 26 stands in this tradition, understanding holiness at least as much in terms of what and whom one avoids as in terms of what and whom one embraces.

Yet we have to be careful with this approach, because the teaching of Jesus tells us that the identity of the righteous is not always clear (Matthew 13.29; 25.32-40), and he was famous for associating himself with 'sinners' (see, for example, Luke 15.2).

In fact, like Jesus, the psalmist offers us the clue to identifying the right way. It is to understand that the glory that illuminates his path and allows his foot to stand firm (v.12) is the loving-kindness (the *hesed*) of the Lord. We need to fix our eyes on this, and as we fix our eyes, so our hearts will be moved to respond likewise in love (v.8).

Reflection by **Joanna Collicutt**

Refrain: *Lord, I love the place where your glory abides.*

Prayer: *Have mercy on us and redeem us, O Lord,*
for our merits are your mercies
and in your judgement is our salvation;
through Jesus Christ our Lord.

PSALM 26

Psalm 27

**The Lord is my light and my salvation;
whom then shall I fear?**

'Your face, Lord, will I seek' (v.10)

The people of God are not insulated from the troubles of the world. Indeed, sometimes we find that the world is against us because of our witness to the ways of God.

Real danger and terrifying threats run throughout the psalm. Enemies are round about, false witnesses breathe out violence, and even father and mother may reject those whom they once held dear. The psalmist neither denies the dangers nor dismisses the threats but rather faces them down with a believing heart and a prayerful life.

When it feels as if everything is against us, that there are forces that would even eat up our flesh (v.2), the psalm calls us to believe in God's goodness, to pray for God's deliverance and always to seek God's face.

The face of God – the true identity and awesome reality of God – is revealed in the face of Jesus Christ who proves that God is our 'light and salvation' by defeating the enemy of death that encamps against us (v.3) and raising us into the 'house of the Lord'.

In that place of the presence of God, where we can see the beauty of the Lord, we not only find solace and safety in time of trouble, but also gain strength to live life fully and to overcome the discordant noise of a disturbed world with our music of praise to the God who offers light to everyone and wills salvation for all.

Reflection by **Christopher Cocksworth**

PSALM 27

Refrain: *The Lord is my light and my salvation*

Prayer: *God, our light and our salvation,
illuminate our lives,
that we may see your goodness in the land
of the living,
and, looking on your beauty,
may be changed into the likeness of Jesus Christ
our Lord.*

To you I call, O Lord my rock;
be not deaf to my cry...

'... shepherd them and carry them for ever' (v.11)

Shepherds sometimes say that the crook they carry in the fields is not best used to hook naughty lambs with but to place so deep in the earth that they can hold on to it, keeping themselves so still that eventually the sheep learn to trust them. This psalm ends with the image of God as shepherd, and you sense that the poet has learned that, unlike some people who speak words at odds with whom they are and what they intend (v.3), God is the depth from whom authenticity, integrity and wisdom can be drawn and trusted: 'my heart has trusted in him and I am helped' (v.8).

The biblical scholar Walter Brueggemann has said that 'the psalms are worship texts without the stage directions'. Psalms were used in ancient worship, but we no longer know quite how they developed such mood swings as those as we find in the psalms of lament, of which this is a good example. It moves from a crisis of human bad behaviour and a petition for safety (vv.1-6) to a clear statement that prayer has been heard and that the heart can now dance for joy (vv.7-11). God hatches a freshness in us and in our shared lives. This literary or liturgical motif simply reflects the truth that in God all our hard full stops in life are turned into commas. He loves us just as we are, but he loves us so much that he doesn't want us to stay like that.

Reflection by **Mark Oakley**

Refrain: The Lord is my strength and my shield.

Prayer: Hear us, Shepherd of your people,
forgive us our sins
and, in a world of pretences,
make us true in heart and mind;
through Jesus Christ our Lord.

PSALM 28

Psalm 29

**Ascribe to the Lord, you powers of heaven,
ascribe to the Lord glory and strength.**

'The Lord sits enthroned above the water flood' (v.9)

With surprising confidence, the psalmist commands the greatest powers in the created universe to bow down and worship God. He is like the priest of creation, telling his congregation (the 'powers') to kneel and pray.

This is a God worthy of such worship because he exceeds all created powers. The psalm shows us this excess in two ways. First, in an almighty firework display – a contest of strength in which the voice of God matches anything that the world can do in its own power. This voice has immense and terrifying might and immense and terrifying precision; it can make land leap up into the air (v.6), and can split lightning bolts (v.7). But – as Elijah too discovered when God showed himself to him on Mount Horeb (1 Kings 19) – to know only that God is as big and loud as an earthquake or a storm is not really to know God at all. There is another dimension to the way God exceeds all created powers, of which these fireworks are no more than a pale sign. In a sudden twist of the imagery, we are asked not just to look *at* the water floods, but *above* them. This God is enthroned in an abiding stability and faithfulness that is of a wholly different order to the maelstrom beneath. It endures 'for evermore', and speaks peace.

This, finally, is why honour is due to his name.

Reflection by **Ben Quash**

Refrain: *The Lord shall give his people the blessing of peace.*

Prayer: *Open our ears, glorious Lord Christ,
to hear the music of your voice
above the chaos of this world;
open our eyes to see the vision of your glory,
for you are our King, now and for ever.*

I will exalt you, O Lord,
because you have raised me up
and have not let my foes triumph over me.

'Joy comes in the morning' (v.5)

This psalm is often referred to as a psalm of individual praise and thanksgiving. Indeed, the key theme is praise, and the psalm begins and ends on this note. But, in-between, there is indication of a struggle. It may well be that the author has endured sickness, and has made a recovery. Whatever the situation that lies behind the psalm, the response to the issue that has been faced is to give thanks.

I first encountered this psalm when it appeared in the Lectionary the morning after a particularly challenging evening. In the midst of the turmoil of that time, the phrase that struck me as most resonant was the idea that joy comes in the morning. Whereas for some the night is a time of sleep and rest, for others the night represents fear and trouble. The idea that things really do seem better in daylight is perhaps a resonant contemporary – and in many ways, timeless – representation of these ancient words. Yet what is also striking in this psalm is the very intimate relationship between the psalmist and the Lord to whom it is directed.

The Hebrew text that lies behind our translation is incredibly terse; it evokes a deep and raw sense of emotion. Nothing is hidden from God, and God is found in the midst of the distress as well as in the deliverance from it.

Reflection by **Helen-Ann Hartley**

Refrain: *You brought me up, O Lord, from the dead.*

Prayer: *Lord, you hide your face*
when we trust in ourselves;
strip us of false security
and re-clothe us in your praise,
that we may know you
as the one who raises us from death,
as you raised your Son, our Saviour Jesus Christ.

PSALM 30

Psalm 31

**In you, O Lord, have I taken refuge;
let me never be put to shame.**

'I have become like a broken vessel' (v.12)

Sometimes things are so important they need saying twice. Psalm 31 has that echoing structure. In the first eight verses a cry for help (vv.1-5) is followed by a deliberate song of trust and affirmation (vv.6-8). Perhaps on some days, these first eight verses will be enough to restore us in trouble and give us perspective in affliction. The longer half of the psalm is for the other days: the days when trouble and sorrow accumulate, and it is harder to find the light.

The lament is deeper now and the language is stronger: grief, sighing, affliction, reproach and dread. I am forgotten and broken. Distress is compounded by gloating enemies. The prayer for deliverance is more urgent. Anxiety overflows into a desire for retribution.

But this inner storm has its conclusion also in the final (and again deeper) song of trust (vv.19-24). In the temple liturgy, perhaps there was a prophetic word, a ritualized word of assurance. A minister would offer grace and comfort.

As we say the psalm today, alone or with others, the gale of our distress surfaces to be heard and held; our fears are named; our anger finds release. Slowly perspective and trust return. We rediscover God's presence in his absence. We find confidence once again, in the final verses, to encourage others as we have ourselves received his grace.

Reflection by **Steven Croft**

Refrain: *Into your hands I commend my spirit.*

Prayer: *Lord Jesus Christ,
when scorn and shame besiege us
and hope is veiled in grief,
hold us in your wounded hands
and make your face shine on us again,
for you are our Lord and God.*

PSALM 31

**Happy the one whose transgression is forgiven,
and whose sin is covered.**

'... you forgave the guilt of my sin' (v.6)

'Sorry' is an easy word to say, but we often take a long time to get round to it. The psalmist has delayed far too long. Unacknowledged shame and guilt have hung heavily upon him. His body has wasted away; he is groaning all day long.

Of course not all sickness is the result of our sins. Illness may come simply because the world is not as it should be – it has been genetically modified by the sin of Adam.

Sometimes the state of our relationships can affect our health. If we are out of sorts with God or with other people, it is not surprising we are out of sorts with ourselves.

At other times it can be the shame or bitterness left by unforgiven sin, and an unforgiving spirit that brings us low. The good news in Jesus Christ is that we can be forgiven, and learn to forgive. Within God's love there is a safe place where we can find healing and deliverance. This psalmist speaks of the happiness of the sinner, forgiven by God – covering the sin and putting it out of sight.

As my father used to say: 'God covers forgiven sinners for all eternity with the robe of righteousness, which is Jesus Christ.'

Of course we are often too stubborn to notice God's call to forgive and be forgiven. Like angry mules, we posture and strut until the truth dawns on us – that we are surrounded by God's steadfast love, so we can rejoice!

Reflection by **John Sentamu**

Refrain: *Be glad, you righteous, and rejoice in the Lord.*

Prayer: *Give us honest hearts, O God,
and send your kindly Spirit
to help us confess our sins
and bring us the peace of your forgiveness;
in Jesus Christ our Lord.*

PSALM 32

Psalm 33

Rejoice in the Lord, O you righteous,
for it is good for the just to sing praises.

'The Lord looks down from heaven; he sees all humankind' (v.13)

Strange though it may seem, one of the great comforts that the psalms offer is a quality we too often take for granted: perspective. By this, I mean that perspective allows you to stand apart from imminent crises, apparent despair or seeming hopelessness, and begin to see things as God might see them – against the background of time and history; in the context of the whole of humanity; not limited by time or space. We as people act locally, and sometimes think globally. God, however, is beyond our highest conceptions of universality. And yet – and this is the beauty of God – there is an eye and heart for detail. No sparrow falls, not one hair of your head is lost, without God noticing.

The psalmist writes of God as the one who can cause the waters to be created, yet who can bottle and label the seas. The God who made heaven and earth, and yet watches over all the inhabitants of the earth. The God who stands beyond the earth, and yet who observes all our deeds. Against this, the strength of humanity is nothing. Our hope in the instruments of war cannot prevail against the compassion and might of God. So the psalmist concludes: God is our help and shield. God's steadfastness is stronger than the largest, best-equipped military forces on the planet. Trust in God. Fear God. Be wise, and have some perspective. No ruler is saved by their great army. But the eye of the Lord is on those who fear God and trust in his steadfast love.

Reflection by **Martyn Percy**

Refrain: *The earth is full of the loving-kindness of the Lord.*

Prayer: *Feed your people, Lord,*
with your holy word
and free us from the emptiness of our wrongful desires,
that we may sing the new song of salvation
through Jesus Christ our Lord.

PSALM 33

**I will bless the Lord at all times;
his praise shall ever be in my mouth.**

'Look upon him and be radiant' (v.5)

Like a number of the psalms, this one begins with thanksgiving and blessing which then opens out into testimony, reflection and teaching. It is notable for the particular joy of the opening and the call to fellow worshippers to find the same healing from fear and shame that this sufferer has found. By seeking the face of God, the 'poor soul' is lifted beyond his troubles into a place of security, protected by the angel of God's presence.

The psalm could have ended at verse 10, but it goes on to invite others to learn from the experience of deliverance. A life lived in the fear of the Lord is a life of promise and fulfilment. Verses 13 to 15 are quoted at the beginning of the rule of St Benedict as an invitation to all who seek the good life to find it by trusting in God and pursuing goodness and truth. Though those who choose the good life are not spared suffering, their prayers will always be heard and their final deliverance is assured.

The 20th verse was taken by the early Christians as a prophecy that Jesus would die on the cross without having his legs broken, but in this context it speaks of God's intimate care for those who trust him.

Reflection by **Angela Tilby**

Refrain: *O taste and see that the Lord is gracious.*

Prayer: *Send your holy angels
to watch over us, O God,
that on our lips will be found your truth
and in our hearts your love;
so we may ever taste your goodness
in the land of the living;
through Jesus Christ our Lord.*

Psalm 35, vv.1-10

Contend, O Lord, with those that contend with me; fight against those that fight against me.

'... say to my soul, "I am your salvation" ' (v.3)

In an argument in the playground, people always wanted the big lad on their side. So did the psalmist. Without any reason or provocation there were people hiding a net or digging a pit for the innocent psalmist to fall into. No wonder he wanted God to make their way dark and slippery (v.6). He wanted them soundly shamed and disgraced (v.4). I know the feeling. When that driver cuts me up, I have several ideas for his subsequent entertainment.

But if we look for retribution and a balancing of the scales in this life, we will be severely disappointed. It is rather more important that we attend to ourselves and how we will respond to misfortune rather than that we plot how God should take the other person behind the bike sheds and sort him out. Following the rule of an eye for an eye and a tooth for a tooth leads to a world that's blind and toothless.

Let's just come clean – life isn't fair and it's no use complaining about it. Too often in misfortune we indulge ourselves with a whinge and a prayer. But Jesus was very clear eyed about the way to face life's sharp edges; you take them to a cross and let God deal with them. After all, God is the one who knows about resurrection.

Look out for resurrection today.

Reflection by **John Pritchard**

PSALM 35

Refrain: Give me justice, O Lord my God,
according to your righteousness.

Prayer: Free us, righteous God, from all oppression,
and bring justice to the nations,
that all the world may know you
as King of kings and Lord of lords,
now and for ever.

**False witnesses rose up against me;
they charged me with things I knew not.**

*'Awake, arise, to my cause,
to my defence, my God and my Lord!' (v.24)*

The accusation that God is asleep is not uncommon. God is often much too quiet for our liking. It's all very well being told that God doesn't pull levers to control things that are going wrong, nor shout loudly to force people to listen to him. It's fine that God is modest, humble even, but surely there are limits? 'Give me justice, O Lord my God, according to your righteousness; let them not triumph over me' (v.25). I need someone to stand up for me for once.

The further we go on the Christian journey, however, the more we realize that God doesn't promise safety, prosperity or even spiritual highs. God promises to be with us. Just that. God promises to be with us wherever we go, in absolutely every circumstance. And my memory of being a child was that what made the difference in every scary situation was simply the presence of a parent.

And as God is life, hope, love, or what spiritual writer Richard Rohr calls 'unfettered resurrection', I reckon God's promise to be with me is actually all I need. God's presence may be quieter than we'd like, but it's as solid as anything we'll ever know. The trick is to lean on that truth (that is, to trust it) all through today. And then again tomorrow. It's called 'practising the presence of God'. And it works.

Reflection by **John Pritchard**

Refrain: Give me justice, O Lord my God,
      according to your righteousness.

Prayer: Free us, righteous God, from all oppression,
     and bring justice to the nations,
     that all the world may know you
     as King of kings and Lord of lords,
     now and for ever.

PSALM 35

Psalm 36

**Sin whispers to the wicked, in the depths of their heart;
there is no fear of God before their eyes.**

'Your love, O Lord, reaches to the heavens' (v.5)

From the opening of this psalm it is clear that the author has no
illusions: sin is a deep and ever-present reality, which holds 'the
wicked' in its vice-like grip. It is a creeping, insidious horror, which
'whispers' to the wicked in the depths of their hearts (v.1), inciting
them to evil and blinding them to goodness (vv.2-4).

But set against this is a triumphant affirmation of faith: 'Your love,
O Lord, reaches to the heavens and your faithfulness to the clouds'
(v.5). The psalmist introduces a strong vigorous motif in verse 9: the
idea of God as 'the well of life', with its suggestion of energy, health
and limitless nourishment. This image was used by Jesus to powerful
effect in his encounter with the woman of Samaria at Jacob's well:
'The water that I will give will become…a spring of water gushing
up to eternal life' (John 4.14). Christian poets also have been drawn
to this theme: in his poem 'The Well', the Welsh priest/poet Euros
Bowen wrote of the human heart as 'a well by the wayside… its
source a trust in bright waters'.

In our view of the world, we tend to swing between amnesia and
despair. As we continue to live with the consequences of human sin,
we need to pray for God's protection (v.11), and each day renew our
hope and trust by drinking from the 'well of life'.

Reflection by **Barbara Mosse**

PSALM 36

Refrain: *With you, O God, is the well of life.*

Prayer: *O God, the well of life,
make us bright with wisdom,
that we may be lightened with the knowledge of your
glory
in the face of Jesus Christ our Lord.*

**Fret not because of evildoers;
be not jealous of those who do wrong.**

'... he will give you your heart's desire' (v.4)

If faith is about orienting ourselves Godwards and aligning ourselves with his nature (see reflection on Psalm 5, p.22), trust is about continuing on that way even when there are no apparent benefits and some obvious costs.

Like Jesus, the psalmist enjoins his hearers not to worry or become discouraged by what they see around them – the apparent triumph of evil over good. Instead, they are to remember that things can always be seen differently. They can be seen from another angle or, as in this case, in terms of a different time-frame. The perspective they and we are required to take is not only a heavenly perspective; it is an ultimate perspective.

For the psalmist and his people, this is a long game, one that involves patience and endurance, which are in their turn supported by an attitude of sitting somewhat lightly to the challenges of our present situation, always aware that it is a provisional state of affairs.

This psalmist has the gift of old age, which helps him take this longer-term view. As we age, our bodies weaken, and as the end of life approaches, there can be an opening up of spiritual awareness (sometimes referred to as 'gerotranscendence'). We realize that the things we were striving for in youth and middle-age are perhaps not so important after all, and we are given the opportunity of recalibrating our priorities. We can find that our heart's desire is not quite what we thought – prosperity, social success, legacy – but instead that our hearts are restless for their eternal rest in God.

Reflection by **Joanna Collicutt**

Refrain: *The salvation of the righteous comes from the Lord.*

Prayer: *Blessed and holy God,
ever merciful and forgiving,
may we turn from what is evil
and do what is good in your sight,
for you have saved us by the cross of your Son,
our Saviour Jesus Christ.*

PSALM 37

Psalm 37, vv.21-end

**The wicked borrow and do not repay,
but the righteous are generous in giving.**

'Wait upon the Lord and keep his way' (v.35)

The ancient Israelites were able to sustain trust in God by recalling his mighty deeds of salvation in previous times. For Christians, this trust is based on God's decisive act of salvation in Christ. For us the demand – and it is a great demand – is to trust that, with the coming, death and resurrection of Jesus, things really did change irrevocably, that the ultimate has broken into the now, and that the meek are inheriting the earth (v.11; cf. Matthew 5.5).

We are called to watch for the breaking in of God's kingdom and to eagerly await its full consummation when Jesus returns. But this is an active dynamic rather than a passive static watching and waiting (see reflection on Psalm 5, p.22). We watch and wait by walking the way of Christ, a paradoxical action summed up well by the Greek word *sēteō*, often translated as 'seek' (as, for example, in Matthew 6.33). Where we find God at work in the world, we join in.

Christian moral teaching is essentially based on the idea that we are poised between the times and should live as ones who await the coming of Jesus to judge the world. This is not so much because we don't want him to catch us out behaving badly, but simply that for the Christian to wait for Christ boils down to living a Christ-like life (Titus 2.11-14). And we do not wait alone and comfortless (John 14.15-17); the Spirit is with us to illuminate, sustain and empower us.

Reflection by **Joanna Collicutt**

Refrain: *The salvation of the righteous comes from the Lord.*

Prayer: *Blessed and holy God,
ever merciful and forgiving,
may we turn from what is evil
and do what is good in your sight,
for you have saved us by the cross of your Son,
our Saviour Jesus Christ.*

**Rebuke me not, O Lord, in your anger,
neither chasten me in your heavy displeasure.**

'... you will answer me, O Lord my God' (v.15)

It's amazing, in the midst of this utterly dark psalm – a psalm that has been described as 'all passion and no resurrection' – to find this trusting assertion, 'you will answer me, O Lord my God!' (v.15). You would have thought the litany of complaint here was unanswerable: the physical pain of festering wounds; the mental agony of deep depression, 'I go about mourning all the day long' (v.6); and then not even the sympathy of neighbours but, on the contrary, social ostracism, with friends and companions standing far off. And to cap it all, there is the intolerable sense of spiritual oppression, the sense that all this has somehow been inflicted by God, that far from binding up our wounds, he is shooting us with arrows. How will the Lord answer that?

He answers in the strangest and deepest way. The psalmist already intuits that somehow the Lord 'knows all' our desires, that our sighing is 'not hidden' (v.9), but how? We, reading this psalm in the dark light of the cross, suddenly see it all: 'I am ... like one who is dumb, who does not open his mouth' (v.13). Isaiah 53.7 echoes this, and both passages take us straight to Christ, standing with us, for us, in us, in the midst of this otherwise unanswerable suffering. No wonder the psalm ends with Christ's title: 'Lord of my salvation'.

Reflection by **Malcolm Guite**

Refrain: *Make haste to help me,
O Lord of my salvation.*

Prayer: *Almighty Lord and Saviour,
behold with pity the wounds of your people;
do not forsake us, sinful as we are,
but for the sake of the passion of your
    Beloved One, Jesus,
come quickly to our aid,
for his mercy's sake.*

PSALM 38

Psalm 39

**I said, 'I will keep watch over my ways,
so that I offend not with my tongue.'**

'Turn your gaze from me, that I may be glad again' (v.15)

Psalm 39 abounds with ambiguity and tension. The suffering author vows himself to silence (vv.1-3), but his complaint finally erupts into speech, railing against the transience of life and its apparent futility (vv.6-8). There are resonances here with the outlook of another biblical writer, one who observes the reality of the human condition in similar fashion: 'Vanity of vanities ... What do people gain from all the toil at which they toil under the sun?' (Ecclesiastes 1.2,3). Further resonances can be seen in the book of Job (Psalm 39.11; Job 30.18,19).

After her death in 1997, some of Mother Teresa's journal entries revealed that at times she experienced a sense of 'disconnection' from God. For this, many branded her a hypocrite; one wonders whether Jesus' sense of abandonment by his Father (Matthew 27.46) would be similarly judged!

Real faith must always contain elements of doubt and ambiguity, because now we see only 'in a mirror, dimly' (1 Corinthians 13.12). We are challenged to accept and live with unanswered questions, while, like the psalmist, continuing to affirm that our hope lies in God (v.8). The author concludes, 'Turn your gaze from me, that I may be glad again' (v.15). It is similar to Peter's reaction after Jesus brought in a miraculous catch of fish ('Go away from me, Lord, for I am a sinful man!', Luke 5.8). Neither response betrays atheism, but a humble acknowledgement of the power and mystery of God.

Reflection by **Barbara Mosse**

Refrain: *Lord, let me know my end and the number of my days.*

Prayer: *O Christ, Son of the living God,
help us when we are too cast down to pray,
and grant that we may trust you all our days,
for you are with us in our living and our dying,
Jesus, Lord and God.*

I waited patiently for the Lord;
he inclined to me and heard my cry.

'There is none that can be compared with you' (v.5)

The old Latin translation of this psalm's first verse gave it its shorthand name: *Expectans expectavi*. I expected expectantly.

The psalmist has troubles, and they do not vanish away as the psalm unfolds. If anything, there is a resurgence of them towards the end. But the message is that expecting expectantly is still worth it. This God can provide solid rock for our feet in place of 'the mire and clay' that bogs us down. This God can take the cry from out of our mouths and replace it with song.

The language of this psalm plays with ideas that a later age would call 'sublime': extremes of imagery that dwarf ordinary conception or measurement. The language pushes us to the edge of what our minds can handle. The psalmist declares his sins to be more in number than the hairs of his head. The troubles that have come about him are 'innumerable' too. But, in a countervailing (but equally mind-bending) evocation of abundance, it is declared that God's wonders are more than it is possible to express. Each of these statements takes us into a world where measurement doesn't work any more. Only in a world like this can we begin to appreciate the radical ultimacy as well as the radical intimacy of God, with whom nothing and no one can be compared.

In the one, true God, ultimacy and intimacy are one, and the former resources the latter. This God loves and saves us 'for nothing'.

Reflection by **Ben Quash**

Refrain: *Great are the wonders you have done,*
O Lord my God.

Prayer: *Free us from our sins, O God,*
and may our sacrifices be of praise
to the glory of your Son,
our Redeemer, Jesus Christ.

Psalm 41

Blessed are those who consider the poor and needy;
the Lord will deliver them in the time of trouble.

'... their heart gathers mischief' (v.6)

Too often human beings root their sense of self-worth in the opinions of others. We can come to believe that we only exist if others are applauding. Here in this psalm the author seems to be the victim of a whisper campaign (vv.5-9), and it is troubling his sense of who he is. He finds himself needing to pray to be raised up (v.10) – restored and rehabilitated – because everyone utters 'empty words' about him (v.6).

This is a psalm for our age when adverts, social media and quick-fire reaction can demand of us instant clarity on every possible issue, and reduce our sense of self-worth when others' easy answers fail to notice our deeper complexities and fragility.

Although the psalmist is being pulled around by the gossip of those who think they know him, he knows something more important. First, God blesses those who 'consider the poor', that is, God strengthens those who reflect his own love for those that the world, with its destructive priorities, considers incomplete or lacking (v.1). Second, it is 'integrity' that upholds him in God's eyes (v.12) and not the chattering judgements of the loud or the charm of those who know how to play social games to their own benefit. When we are tempted to live down to the voices of others, God sets us before his face (v.12) so that we can hear his voice, living up to it and being raised up (v.10).

Reflection by **Mark Oakley**

PSALM 41

Refrain: *O Lord, be merciful to me.*

Prayer: *God our deliverer,*
raise up the poor and comfort the betrayed,
through the one who for our sakes became poor
and whose betrayal brought our salvation,
Jesus Christ our Lord.

**As the deer longs for the water brooks,
so longs my soul for you, O God.**

'Why have you forgotten me?' (v.11)

We tend to romanticize the Psalms. Several times this one has been turned into a hymn about contented countryside animals. Actually, it is about an emaciated deer scraping its carcass through the desert dustbowl in desperation. Why was the psalmist so desolate? Because all the evidence seemed to be that God had abandoned him.

If you have ever felt like that, three things the psalmist did might help. First, he kept crying out to God, even though he was not sure that God was listening (v.7). Second, he went back in mind to a time when he did have assurance of God's presence, remembering songs of worship from his past (vv.4–5). Third, he was totally honest with God and told it like it was – angry and confused (v.3).

That honesty brought him a reward. Suddenly he had a stunning and reassuring glimpse of God. In the barren heights of Mount Mizar he had a vision of water cascading all over him (v.9). He was overwhelmed by hope in God's loving-kindness (v.10). No sooner than it had come, it was gone. He was back to anguish, but for an undeniable moment it was there.

So when the writer says, 'put your trust in God' (v.14), this isn't a platitude that comes from an untroubled heart. He says it because old habits are still valuable, even after they have stopped feeling refreshing.

Reflection by **Peter Graystone**

Refrain: *vv.6-7, repeated at vv.13-14*

Prayer: *Come, creator Spirit, source of life;
sustain us when our hearts are heavy
and our wells have run dry,
for you are the Father's gift,
with him who is our living water,
Jesus Christ our Lord.*

Psalm 43

Give judgement for me, O God,
and defend my cause against an ungodly people.

'You are the God of my refuge' (v.2)

Following on closely from its predecessor (some commentators even say that psalms 42 and 43 were originally one complete psalm; note the repetition of the phrase in v.5), this psalm speaks of lament. This is a prayer that speaks of the gulf between despair and praise. That the two are ultimately linked together is remarkable, and serves as a reminder that any relationship with God is inevitably made up of both extremes.

We cannot have one without the other. Life in its totality is surely full of both aspects. The image of God as refuge in v.2 is an anchor point for the whole psalm, but its meaning is wider than a place of safety and retreat. One of the fascinating things about the psalms is that they are proclaimed in the fullness of life, that even at the times of being tested, there is a willingness to face matters head on.

Refuge is more accurately imagined as strength for the journey, rather than escape and retreat. To feel protected is one matter, but to feel strengthened at the very point of trial is at the heart of the psalmist's prayer. Linked to praise, it speaks of a sense of confidence that putting one's trust in God yields results far beyond that which we ever thought possible.

Reflection by **Helen-Ann Hartley**

Refrain: vv.5-6

Prayer: *Come, creator Spirit, light and truth;*
bring us to the altar of life
and renew our joy and gladness
in Jesus Christ our Lord.

**We have heard with our ears, O God, our forebears
have told us,
all that you did in their days, in time of old.**

'... you have rejected us and brought us to shame' (v.10)

To begin with, it all seemed so simple. In Psalm 1 things were presented as a very distinct either/or choice; and the writer was quite clear that righteousness brings the Lord's blessing, wickedness his curse (Psalm 1.1,6). But in today's psalm something has clearly gone wrong with this understanding. In verses 1 to 9 the writer is reminding God of all that he did for the Israelite people 'in time of old' (v.1), and how he continued to empower his people in the writer's own time (vv.5-9).

But the victories Israel once enjoyed are long gone, so the psalmist assumes that God has rejected his people. His sense of injury and indignation is palpable as he declares, 'All this has come upon us, though we have not forgotten you, and have not played false to your covenant' (v.18). The only explanation for the author is that God must have gone to sleep, and in the concluding verses the psalmist urges God to wake and come to Israel's aid.

Israel's growth in understanding of the mysterious ways of God took many generations to evolve. For each one of us also, it may well take a lifetime to fully embrace the truth of Jesus' teaching: 'Love your enemies ... for [God] makes his sun rise on the evil and the good, and sends rain on the righteous and on the unrighteous' (Matthew 5.44-45).

Reflection by **Barbara Mosse**

Refrain: *Rise up, O Lord, to help us.*

Prayer: *In the darkness of unknowing,*
when your love seems absent,
draw near to us, O God,
in Christ forsaken,
in Christ risen,
our Redeemer and our Lord.

PSALM 44

Psalm 45

My heart is astir with gracious words;
as I make my song for the king,
my tongue is the pen of a ready writer.

'... therefore shall the peoples praise you for ever and ever' (v.17)

Long before the days of wedding photographs, this psalm was written to preserve the memory of a wonderful day in the life of a family and of a nation – a royal wedding. There are several snapshots in the slideshow for the day:

- The handsome groom, dressed like a guardsman, sword at his side, riding on horseback to the ceremony, like a conquering hero.
- The royal sceptre – a gleaming symbol of righteousness and justice, of true integrity, and of God-given responsibility.
- Happiness writ large on the face of the king, and his fine clothes sweet smelling, fragrant with spices.
- The young queen-to-be, dressed in gold, surrounded by nobles from far and near – with a mixture of trust and anxiety in her face, as she leaves her people and her father's house, for the new life to come.
- The bridesmaids following on in all their finery too. What a celebration!
- The big moment – when the bride and her party enter the palace of the king. Her new home, for ever!
- The king is praised in language exclusively reserved for God!

For St Paul, marriage was a picture of the even more important relationship that there is between Christ and his Church (Ephesians 5.25ff). Think of the snapshots described above. If you were putting together an album of pictures to celebrate Christ and his Church, what pictures would you choose?

Reflection by **John Sentamu**

Refrain: *Behold our defender, O God,*
and look upon the face of your anointed.

Prayer: *Lord our God,*
bring your bride, your holy Church,
with joy to the marriage feast of heaven,
and unite us with your anointed Son,
Jesus Christ our Lord.

PSALM 45

**God is our refuge and strength,
a very present help in trouble.**

'Come and behold the works of the Lord' (v.8)

In times of distress we try to trust God, but it's so difficult when we can't actually see him intervening. The psalmist knew that. He wrote about Jerusalem being shaken by an earthquake, but that the river which flowed through it was a sign of God's presence (v.4).

You've been tricked! There never was such a river. It was and is an invisible river, detectable only with the eyes of faith. That river is God himself. Those who recognize it need not fear (v.2).

This is a psalm to return to repeatedly as our lives and our world pass through crises, which then become history. It speaks of how the God who sustained us in the past is the same God who will not let us down in the present.

We've flooded the bathroom and the world did not come to an end, and neither did our faith. We've fallen disastrously in love with all the wrong people, and we are still alive – and so is Jesus. We've lost our jobs and our car keys and our health and our tempers, and God is still bearing us up.

Our doubts and fears are not at an end. But we can overcome difficulties because of the absolute commitment of the Lord of Hosts to be with us (v.11). And with that in mind, I suggest we all take a moment to be still and know that the Lord is God (v.10).

Reflection by **Peter Graystone**

Refrain: *The Lord of hosts is with us;
the God of Jacob is our stronghold.*

Prayer: *God of Jacob,
when the earth shakes
and the nations are in uproar,
speak, and let the storm be still;
through Jesus Christ our Lord.*

PSALM 46

Psalm 47

Clap your hands together, all you peoples;
O sing to God with shouts of joy.

'Sing praises to God, sing praises' (v.6)

Christianity, it is often said, is a singing faith. We cannot simply do justice to our religion by speaking well, believing right or doing good. We sing. And when we sing, something happens to us. Parts of our heart, mind and body that are often not used begin to offer something to God – and to one another – that words and actions alone cannot achieve. When we sing, we stand, sit or kneel differently. We pray differently; we breathe differently.

The Christian who sings, said Augustine, prays twice. But why? Because singing involves us all; it is one of those activities where you can't easily hold back. We give our all as our lungs and mouths open in praise. Not everyone can pray or speak lucidly, but most can sing with great gusto. Few can play a musical instrument with beauty and precision, but everyone can make a noise in celebration.

Jean Vanier, the founder of L'Arche, says God became small in our world, in order to teach us to love and be open to those who are often overlooked. Through his friendship with a priest named Thomas Philippe, Vanier became aware of the plight of thousands of people with developmental disabilities, often shut away in institutions. Vanier sought to set them free, and live in communities where they could express themselves more fully. The L'Arche Community is often known for its singing. Because the God of tenderness who loves us, raises us all up so that we can all be instruments of his praise.

Reflection by **Martyn Percy**

Refrain: *O sing praises to God, sing praises.*

Prayer: *As Christ was raised by your glory, O Father,*
so may we be raised to new life
and rejoice to be called your children,
both now and for ever.

PSALM 47

**Great is the Lord and highly to be praised,
in the city of our God.**

'God has established her for ever' (v.8)

This is a ceremonial psalm in praise of Jerusalem: its city, mountain and temple, which represent God's dwelling place on earth. Jerusalem is the link between earth and heaven, between earthly worship and the divine presence. The central section describes an assault on the city, which fails because the assailants simply lose heart when they realize the glory and strength of what God has established. The link God has forged with earth through the city and its temple is established for ever and cannot be broken. Yet, in Jewish and Christian memory, the Zion of this psalm did not last for ever. The temple was destroyed and the city plundered more than once.

Christians can now read this psalm in the light of the coming of Christ and the new covenant that is established by his death and resurrection in the Holy City. Christ is the sacrament of God's presence on earth. He is the sanctuary, the place of refuge. The worship we offer on earth prepares us for the worship of heaven, but it also enables us to see the whole earth in the light of God's justice revealed in Christ.

Our task today is to witness to God's faithfulness and to ensure that, just as God revealed himself in ancient Zion, so his wisdom and majesty are proclaimed to the next generation.

Reflection by **Angela Tilby**

Refrain: *We have waited on your loving-kindness, O God.*

Prayer: *Father of lights,
raise us with Christ to your eternal city,
that, with kings and nations,
we may wait in the midst of your temple
and see your glory for ever and ever.*

PSALM 48

Psalm 49

Hear this, all you peoples;
listen, all you that dwell in the world...

'My heart shall meditate on understanding' (v.3)

In *The New Interpreter's Bible*, the theologian J. Clinton McCann comments that our twenty-first-century economy has moved way beyond the simple principle of supply and demand, and is now designed 'not to meet people's needs but to stimulate people's greed'. The saying, 'you can't take it with you' is one with which we are all familiar, and this psalm makes it clear that the human tendency to fret over wealth and riches is as old as humanity itself (vv.5,6,17).

The psalm begins with a clarion call to the whole of humanity, 'of low or high degree, both rich and poor together' (v.2). This is what the world is like, implies the author; accept it, get used to it – and rise above it. This isn't easy, but the first step is to seek God's wisdom before all else (v.3). This is totally consistent with Jesus' teaching, when he urges his disciples to 'strive first for the kingdom of God' (Matthew 6.33). If God truly is the disciple's first priority, then there is no need for envy or worry; everything else in life will assume its rightful place and perspective.

And there are other resonances. In one of the post-resurrection appearances, Peter asks Jesus about the future of the beloved disciple (John 21.21). Jesus' reply is, in effect, 'Mind your own business! Follow me!' (John 21.22). How good are we at following Jesus' advice?

Reflection by **Barbara Mosse**

PSALM 49

Refrain: *Blessed is the one who trusts in the Lord.*

Prayer: *Save us from envy, God our Redeemer,*
and deliver us from the chains of wealth,
that, ransomed through your Son,
we may inherit the crown of everlasting life;
through Jesus Christ our Lord.

**The Lord, the most mighty God, has spoken
and called the world from the rising of the sun to its setting.**

'... should I keep silence?' (v.21)

Although some of the psalms question why God is silent, here God speaks quite clearly and very uncomfortably. In the midst of the poem's call to worship, there are two direct addresses by God, in verses 7-15 and verses 16-23. Verse 4 tells us that God is calling his people together so that he can judge them. We often associate the idea of judgement in the scriptures with condemnation, punishment and retribution. However, when God's people are judged, it is more usually to help them see who they have become, to enable their liberation from those things that control and shape us all without us even knowing.

In this psalm God reminds those who have committed to a relationship with him in a covenant that sometimes the hardest hearts to convert are those of the converted. He has to remind them that often the more busily religious they are, the less faithful they become; the more they ritually 'perform' their faith, the more obscured can be their spiritual motivation. The same lips that recite God's statutes can go on to belittle and harm those we share life with (vv. 16-20). The best way to get back on track in this spiritual chaos is to focus again on gratitude because it opens up the heart again to the God who 'shines forth' (v.2). 'You that forget God, consider this well' (v.23) is the psalm's summarised lesson in self-scrutiny for the worshipper.

Reflection by **Mark Oakley**

Refrain: *Offer to God a sacrifice of thanksgiving.*

Prayer: *Mighty God,*
dwelling in unapproachable light,
forgive our vain attempts to appease you,
and show us your full salvation
in Jesus Christ your Son our Lord.

PSALM 50

73

Psalm 51

**Have mercy on me, O God, in your great goodness;
according to the abundance of your compassion
blot out my offences.**

'Cleanse me from my sin' (v.2)

Any mention of the word 'sin' is bound to draw up a plethora of images and presuppositions. This psalm speaks of a profound understanding of sin and forgiveness. The misinterpretation of verse 6 – 'I have been wicked even from my birth, a sinner when my mother conceived me' – has led to some unfortunate conclusions. It does not speak about original sin, nor of the uncleanness of intimacy, but rather places the writer in the midst of an acknowledgement that he is part of a sinful people, whose misdeeds have perpetuated down many generations.

The result of all of this is alienation from God, which is perhaps the greatest punishment of all. The desire in the psalm for cleansing is not so much about self-purity, but a need to be reconnected with God. When relationships are broken, we feel the pain of separation. When they are restored, we feel wholly renewed and refreshed. In this psalm, the petition for forgiveness, cleansing and renewal leads to confession and thanksgiving. God is petitioned to rebuild the walls of Jerusalem in order that sacrifices might be offered once more.

The rebuilding that represents the process of forgiveness is done with the knowledge of God's grace. If we can hold on to this assurance, then any act of repentance must surely be a joyful one. This psalm is thus notable for its persistent gladness in the face of the pain of sin.

Reflection by **Helen-Ann Hartley**

Refrain: *The sacrifice of God is a broken spirit.*

Prayer: *Take away, good Lord, the sin that corrupts us;
give us the sorrow that heals
and the joy that praises
and restore by grace your own image within us,
that we may take our place among your people;
in Jesus Christ our Lord.*

PSALM 51

Why do you glory in evil, you tyrant,
while the goodness of God endures continually?

'... like a spreading olive tree' (v.8)

Sometimes the truth pierces us, but it's usually falsehood that cuts us up. So with the tyrant here, whose tongue is like a sharpened razor. Whoever the tyrant was then, we know our own tyrants only too well: the many mouths of the all-pervasive advertisers, trying to get us to glory in evil. Theirs are the razor tongues that cut all the old rooted virtues to ribbons with their mockery: faithfulness, prudence, any rootedness or quiet content, modesty and gentleness are all seen as old-fashioned or hypocritical or repressed or prudish, all slashed at with the sharpened tongue and the hurtful word, all bonds and gestures, pushed aside, as Larkin says, like an outdated combine harvester. And instead the tyrants tell us we are to trust in great riches and to rely on the wickedness by which they are mostly made.

What a great moment of freedom and rebellion it is then to recite this psalm. We find ourselves centred on the simple fruitful image of the olive tree, not uprooted and torn up as the psalmist knows that false life will surely be, but rooted instead, deeply and simply in God's everlasting goodness, unhurried by the time-driven bullies snapping at our heels, taking time for that slow growth that will bear real fruit in the olives of mercy and peace and in that quiet delight that no one will ever sell or buy.

Reflection by **Malcolm Guite**

Refrain: *I trust in the goodness of God for ever and ever.*

Prayer: *Faithful and steadfast God,*
nourish your people in this wicked world,
and, through prayer and the Scriptures,
give us our daily bread;
through Jesus Christ our Lord.

PSALM 52

Psalm 53

The fool has said in his heart, 'There is no God.'
Corrupt are they, and abominable in their wickedness;
 there is no one that does good.

'Have they no knowledge?' (v.4)

Most of the psalms are prayers and praises addressed to God, but a few of them take the form of reflection on life in God's presence. Here the psalmist muses on the corruption he sees around him.

What might our reflections be? What might we be thinking, in our heart of hearts, when we look around us? We hear stories about people cheating the benefits system and getting money they are not entitled to. Bankers and financiers get big bonuses, we learn, while their customers can hardly make ends meet. Perhaps we do not trust politicians to deliver on their promises. We see communities where the elderly and vulnerable are neglected. We worry about crime and violence in our neighbourhoods. This is what happens, we think, when God is absent, when there are no standards to live up to, and no one watching over the world. We wonder whether God has been ignored and neglected for too long, whether people of faith are too few to make any difference.

Like the psalmist, in the end all we can do is to remember that we are in God's presence when we ask our questions. We know that God is there, concerned about his world, involved with its destiny. So we, like the psalmist, can make our declaration of faith. God will put things right, in his own good time, and then all God's people will rejoice.

Reflection by **Gillian Cooper**

Refrain: *The fear of the Lord is the beginning of wisdom.*

Prayer: *Without you, O God, nothing is real,*
 all things are open to corruption
 and we are deadened by deceit;
 do not abandon us to our folly,
 but give us hearts that seek you
 and, at the last, joy in your heavenly city;
 through Jesus Christ our Lord.

**Save me, O God, by your name
and vindicate me by your power.**

'... praise your name, O Lord, for it is gracious' (v.6)

This is a psalm of vengeance. Modern translations might mitigate this a little by using words like 'vindicate' rather than 'avenge' (in verse 1), but there is no avoiding the context. It wishes evil on its enemies, and downfall, and destruction.

Permission to give vent to these powerful emotions is part of the gift of the book of Psalms as a whole. And as a whole, the book of Psalms also educates our desires, including those that are most entrenched, most bloodthirsty, most obstinate. Here the hatred and hurt of the psalmist are shown already to contain the seeds of a transformation, perhaps even ultimately a purification. Yes, the cry of the psalmist is 'Avenge me!', like a call to a parent or an older sibling to come and announce 'payback time!' to a childhood tormentor. But then there is the tiny but fertile addition 'by your name'. In other words, a chink of recognition is there that this must be on God's terms; it is for the sake of God's name not my own.

This is a psalm in which the 'name' of God is very important: it returns again in verse 6, when it is described as 'gracious' (in older versions, 'so comfortable'; in other words, comforting, healing, forgiving). And if vindication is to be in this so gracious 'name', then it may be as surprising to us as it is to our enemies.

Reflection by **Ben Quash**

Refrain: *Behold, God is my helper.*

Prayer: *O living God,
reach through the violence of the proud
and the despair of the weak
to create in Jesus Christ
a people free to praise your holy name,
now and for ever.*

PSALM 54

Psalm 55

Hear my prayer, O God;
hide not yourself from my petition.

'I am restless in my complaining' (v.2)

The writer here feels under threat and opens with a plea that God will not hide himself from him. The 'voice of the enemy' and 'the clamour of the wicked' surround him (v.3); he feels unequal to the struggle and is in fear for his life (vv.5,6). And the chief source of his pain comes from the fact that the one reviling him is not an obvious enemy, 'for then I could have borne it' (v.13); but 'it was even you, one like myself, my companion and my own familiar friend' (v.15). He longs to escape, to fly away like a bird and make his lodging in the wilderness.

Much of this will have a depressingly familiar ring for us. We, like the writer, experience the 'shifting sands' in our world, which can make even the most apparently trustworthy of relationships difficult to maintain. We, too, may long for escape.

But in the end, the answer for the psalmist is not to run away, but to deepen his roots in God – to establish a rule of life that will sustain him in the face of anything life throws at him. Only God is able to provide this security, and perhaps we, too, are being invited to trust God more deeply. 'Cast your burden upon the Lord and he will sustain you' (v.24).

Reflection by **Barbara Mosse**

Refrain: *Cast your burden upon the Lord and he will sustain you.*

Prayer: *Lord, in all times of fear and dread,*
grant that we may so cast our burdens upon you,
that you may bear us on the holy wings of the Spirit
to the stronghold of your peace;
through Jesus Christ our Lord.

PSALM 55

**Have mercy on me, O God, for they trample over me;
all day long they assault and oppress me.**

'... that I may walk before God in the light of the living' (v.12)

There's an old saying that God plus one makes a majority. We are the one.

The film *Of Gods and Men* tells the true story of a Cistercian monastery in the Atlas mountains where the monks live in fear of terrorists coming and killing them all, as they have done elsewhere. They are very vulnerable, and they know it, but the village around them depends for its safety and well-being on their being there. They have numerous debates about staying or going, but gradually a spirit of Godly confidence and resilience steals over them all and they have a meal, a 'Last Supper', in which joy has the last word. That night the terrorists arrive. The monks are never seen alive again.

'... in God I trust and will not fear, what can flesh do to me?' (v.10) There are worse things than death. The most important thing of all is to know that God is on our side (v.9), and that nothing can separate us from the love of God (Romans 8.39). Given that death never lets you down and remains on call seven days a week, providing an unrivalled round-the-clock service, the important thing is surely what we do with all the stuff we've got that isn't fixed and final – that is, our life. What matters is that I walk before God in the light of the living (v.12). Not just walk, but walk before God.

Quality of life matters more than quantity. Just because it's a truism doesn't mean it isn't true.

Reflection by **John Pritchard**

Refrain: *In God I trust, and will not fear.*

Prayer: *Faithful God,*
  your deliverance is nearer than we know;
  free us from fear
  and help us to find courage in your Word,
  Jesus Christ our Lord.

PSALM 56

Psalm 57

Be merciful to me, O God, be merciful to me,
for my soul takes refuge in you.

'I lie in the midst of lions' (v.5)

Perhaps this psalm really was sung by David as he hid in the cave from Saul (1 Samuel 24.1-7), as some commentators suggest. Whoever is calling out to God here is certainly hiding, in danger from what are characterized both as beasts and as people who tongues are sharp, able to cut to the quick (v.5).

In its two sections, this psalm is really a mini Creed and Gloria: first of all a 'nevertheless' kind of faith, affirming that whatever my circumstances this morning, however low my spirits or isolated my heart, there is always, without fail, somewhere for me to hide until the 'storm of destruction' has passed. It puts into beautiful poetic images the thoroughly human assumption that dominates from time to time, that somehow things are against us, that we are pushing water uphill or wading through treacle – or even more explicitly, that there are *people* who are against us, not on our side, making our life more difficult that it might be. It is in precisely these circumstances that this psalm gives us the words to call out to the God we are not even sure is there. This psalm lets us know that the reason we can't see God at these times is perhaps because we are actually enveloped by the shadow of those wings that give us shelter, so close we can't see them (v.2).

The final verses, repeated near the beginning of Psalm 108, give us a way of thanking God, remembering that God's faithfulness towards us remains, even when we've lost faith in ourselves.

Reflection by **Lucy Winkett**

Refrain: Be exalted, O God, above the heavens,
and your glory over all the earth.

Prayer: Tender God,
gentle protector in time of trouble,
pierce the gloom of despair
and give us, with all your people,
the song of freedom and the shout of praise;
in Jesus Christ our Lord.

Psalm 58

Do you indeed speak justly, you mighty?
Do you rule the peoples with equity?

'... those who speak falsehood go astray' (v.3)

It's possible to sit in front of your TV and be angered by the violence and injustice perpetrated against the innocent and vulnerable. The anger is made worse in your armchair by a sense of powerlessness to act against this evil. This difficult and unusual psalm is born in such rage. The psalmist is outraged by wicked people whose venom can't be charmed away by anyone (v.5), whose lion-like jaws eat into the innocent unless God breaks their fangs (v.6) or evaporates them like water (v.7). Other graphic images continue this theme of 'enough is enough', calling on God to take control so that evil will stop ruining human lives and the world that belongs to God.

The psalm is constructed in three parts. First, the evil are addressed (vv.1-5); then the prayer for justice is made (vv.6-9); at the end assurance is given that because of God goodness is stronger than evil and therefore 'there is a harvest for the righteous' (v.11). At the heart of the trouble, the poet says, is speaking falsehood (v.3). Evil is always caught up in a reckless use of words and self-justifications that creates a distance from reality and can frighteningly curdle into bullying or violent aggression.

The command of Jesus is to love your neighbour as yourself – not hate your neighbour as yourself. In responding to evil in the name of justice, this psalm reminds us, we mustn't unconsciously begin to reflect what we lament. Righteous words can quickly tip into self-righteous ones, and that's when the trouble begins in the soul – and consequently in relationships and the world itself.

Reflection by **Mark Oakley**

Refrain: *The Lord makes himself known by his acts of justice.*

Prayer: *Living God,*
deliver us from a world without justice
and a future without mercy;
in your mercy, establish justice,
and in your justice, remember the mercy
revealed to us in Jesus Christ our Lord.

PSALM 58

Psalm 59

**Rescue me from my enemies, O my God;
set me high above those that rise up against me.**

'To you, O my strength, will I sing' (v.20)

The refrain in Psalm 59 strikes the reader powerfully (vv.7 and 16). Twice we are reminded of the physical danger that faces the psalmist and the community. These enemies are real; they are hungry; they are creatures of darkness. Elsewhere the language of the psalm is of murder, betrayal and violence. Psalm 59 has most often been read as the prayer of a king or some other leader in the midst of a besieged city, looking out on the armies of the enemy and beseeching God for help.

The prayers for help become curses between the two refrains. The psalmist calls down destruction and humiliation on his enemies. Yet the curse is not enough. Hatred cannot overcome these foes. The enemies return.

Psalm 59 is full of violence – but notice where it ends. Not every psalm makes this transition, but in this one, all of this violence is transcended by praise. In the end, even in peril and danger, the psalmist rejoices. Here is an act of determination, an act of the will, to turn away from violence, daily, to meditate on God's mercy and steadfast love, daily, to find strength not in retribution but in grace.

It is no accident that the final word in Psalm 59 (in Hebrew and in English) is love.

Reflection by **Steven Croft**

Refrain: *You, O God, are my strong tower.*

Prayer: *Strong and merciful God,
stand with the oppressed
against the triumph of evil
and the complacency of your people,
and establish in Jesus Christ
your new order of generosity and joy,
for he is alive and reigns now and for ever.*

**O God, you have cast us off and broken us;
you have been angry; restore us to yourself again.**

'I will ... share out the valley of Succoth' (v.6)

God is revealed in this psalm to be a measurer. He plots the dimensions of the land, like a surveyor, and he apportions each lot of land to its tenants, like a landlord. Gilead is his and Manasseh is his.

This same God is revealed in Christian tradition in the form of Jesus, who paces out the earth – travelling from region to region on foot. His footfalls measure the surface of the land – from Galilee to Jerusalem and back again; to Samaria and the regions beyond the river Jordan.

The God who has the measure of all things is the God who apportioned everything its proper place in the great work of creation: the waters above the heavens and the waters below the heavens; the sun and the moon and the stars; the fish in the sea and the birds in the air. He divided and he disposed. But this same God also moves across and within the world whose dimensions he plotted. And he makes a space for us to move in this world with him and in relation to him. We may resist, run away, scatter ourselves or hide ourselves. Or we may gather and walk with him as his disciples, learning to see the earth as he sees it, know it as he knows it, love it as he loves it.

Reflection by **Ben Quash**

Refrain: Restore us again, O God our Saviour.

Prayer: Risen Christ,
you claim your own among the nations;
mend what is broken in us, loving Saviour;
do not forsake us when we fail,
but in your service grant us daring and love;
for your name's sake.

PSALM 60

Psalm 61

Hear my crying, O God,
and listen to my prayer.

'Let me dwell in your tent forever' (v.4)

The Psalms are alarmingly size-ist at times – or so it seems – full of highs and lows; heights and depths. The Psalms seem to proclaim that our sense of hierarchy is all in order. We meet God in the heavens, but in the bowels of the earth all is darkness. And yet, the Psalms also go to great lengths to say that there is nowhere beyond God's reach. God can see through the darkness, because the dark and the light are all the same to him (Psalm 139.12). And whether it seems like a short or a long reach for us to God, God is always nearer than we think. Indeed, he is with us. He never left. He was always close.

This is a psalm of comfort. Each image the psalmist reaches for is one of closeness and containment, of holding and encompassing. We nestle under the wings of God; are led to a rock that is higher; find shelter in the tent of the Lord; are safe in God's tower against an enemy. Whichever image one chooses, God is a refuge – a place of safety, peace and protection.

So, no place or situation is too far away from God's reach. Though we may feel distant, God is close. Though we may stray far, far away, he still abides with us. Though we sense a great distance between ourselves and God – enough for fear and despair to take root – God is always near. And not only near, but near enough to provide a protective, abiding presence. God watches over us.

Reflection by **Martyn Percy**

Refrain: *You are my refuge, O God,*
a strong tower against the enemy.

Prayer: *Risen Christ,*
as you knew the discipline of suffering
and the victory that brings us salvation,
so grant us your presence in our weakness
and a place in your unending kingdom
now and for evermore.

**On God alone my soul in stillness waits;
from him comes my salvation.**

'Wait on God alone in stillness, O my soul' (v.5)

There are times in the spiritual life when faith is put on trial and there is no obvious evidence of God's presence or guidance in our lives. At such times it can be tempting to give up, to abandon our trust in God. This psalm is a call to endurance. The echo of the first line in verse 5 is particularly poignant. We sometimes need to sit it out in God's presence, to wait quietly when all seems against us.

Yet, as the prayer of this psalm progresses, there is a strengthening of faith that comes through sheer dogged persistence. Our prayer brings us to the recognition that everything that is purely human is built on shifting sand. We cannot rely on anything or anyone other than the living God. Gradually we come to realize that God alone provides the security we crave. This recognition brings detachment from the glittering prizes that human beings are prone to pursue.

There is a lesson here for all of us. We should not set our hearts on riches or success, because to do so opens the door to dishonesty and corruption. Only God is worth trusting. He will finally reveal his justice as he returns to us the trust or the treachery with which we have responded to him.

Reflection by **Angela Tilby**

Refrain: *Wait on God alone in stillness, O my soul.*

Prayer: *O God, teach us to seek security,*
not in money or theft,
not in human ambition or malice,
not in our own ability or power,
but in you, the only God,
our rock and our salvation.

PSALM 62

Psalm 63

**O God, you are my God; eagerly I seek you;
my soul is athirst for you.**

'My flesh also faints for you' (v.2)

When babies are born, they are about 78% water. By the time adulthood is reached, that figure has dropped to around 60%. It is an extraordinary statistic. When we look at ourselves in the mirror, we don't naturally think 'water,' and yet, water is vital for life. If we do not have water, we will die. While this psalm is full of confidence, it also contains vulnerability. For this reason, the psalm is often placed in the group of psalms of lament.

The reference to the sanctuary (in verse 3, not apparent in all translations), and to the liars that seek the psalmist's life (in verses 10 and 12) could point to accusations in a criminal setting from which the author seeks to appeal to God's authority and mercy. Underpinning all of this is a confidence that comes from the knowledge of God's ability to sustain.

The image of the sheltering wings is a bold invocation of God's protection. Yet it is the place of drought that represents both the connection to God and the search for God's presence. That balance between certainty and doubt is the hallmark of faith. Times when we are pushed to extremes, when we long for refreshment, are often the times when God has entered our lives in abundance. The opposite of drought, represented by the bold words of verse 6, implies that God's sustenance will be generous in measure.

Reflection by **Helen-Ann Hartley**

PSALM 63

Refrain: *My soul is athirst for God, even for the living God.*

Prayer: *To you we come, radiant Lord,
the goal of all our desiring,
beyond all earthly beauty;
gentle protector, strong deliverer,
in the night you are our confidence;
from first light be our joy;
through Jesus Christ our Lord.*

**Hear my voice, O God, in my complaint;
preserve my life from fear of the enemy.**

'... deep are the inward thoughts of the heart' (v.6)

Who the enemies of the opening verses are is a cause for great speculation in readers of the Psalms, and this may be a reason why sometimes the psychology of the Psalms seems far away from a twenty-first century reader. For people of faith, including the Christian faith, it is often difficult to identify our 'enemies'. Most people think they don't really have any. It may be that the rediscovery of a concept of our 'enemy' might not be such a bad thing, as there will be people in the world, wherever you are reading this, who wish you harm. Either with or without knowing you.

Modern psychology, however, helps us to understand that what we find most challenging in others, including, sometimes, their unfair behaviour towards us, is much more to do with our projection and interpretation than we might have once supposed. In that context, this psalm becomes a personal and profound meditation on the battles that sometimes rage within. Sometimes, taking modern psychological insights into account, our greatest enemy is ourselves, a kind of committee that meets in our heads, ready to scupper our dearest hopes with a unanimous resolution, shuffling their papers, making sure we know that we can't or shouldn't or just won't succeed in the rather tender plans we have made for our lives. The arrows shot at our blameless selves (v.4) come then from the hidden or suppressed parts of our personality, whose eruptions will not be contained unless, as this psalm pleads, God roots them out.

Reflection by **Lucy Winkett**

Refrain: The righteous shall rejoice in the Lord.

Prayer: Cut through the malice of our hearts, redeeming God,
with the Spirit's sword,
wound the pride of our rebellion
with the grace that makes righteous
and bring near the day of Christ,
when love shall reign in joy;
for he is alive and reigns, now and for ever.

PSALM 64

Psalm 65

Praise is due to you, O God, in Zion;
to you that answer prayer shall vows be paid.

'You crown the year with your goodness' (v.11)

The smell of a rural church at Harvest Thanksgiving is, for me, one of life's wonderful nostalgias. I'm thrown instantly into ploughing fields and scattering good seed on the ground, and welcoming small, bewildered children bringing up huge marrows and jars of chutney. The fulfilment of the agricultural year is embedded deep into our psyche, and this psalm catches the mood of thanksgiving and wonder beautifully. Read it again and rejoice!

A master poet is clearly at work. Who else would have thought of saying to God 'your wagon tracks overflow with abundance' or 'the hills gird themselves with joy, the meadows clothe themselves with flocks'? (vv.11-13, ESV) Nor can I resist the translation of the final verse, 'the valleys stand so thick with corn that they shall laugh and sing.' Don't you want to smile?

There is tragedy in nature too. There is drought, earthquake, wind and fire. But these disasters mustn't make us lose the discipline of gratitude for a world of astonishing abundance, created in exuberant colours, anticipated in ravishing smells, and experienced in mouth-watering tastes. Priest and poet G.K. Chesterton said: 'There is but one sin, to call a green leaf grey.' Perhaps today we can determine to notice the green leaf, the greenness of the green and the leafiness of the leaf. And give thanks.

Reflection by **John Pritchard**

Refrain: Be joyful in God, all the earth.

Prayer: May the richness of your creation, Lord,
and the mystery of your providence
lead us to that heavenly city
where all peoples will bring their wealth,
forsake their sins and find their true joy,
Jesus Christ our Lord.

Be joyful in God, all the earth;
sing the glory of his name;
sing the glory of his praise.

'Be joyful ...' (v.1)

It often appears that the psalmist likes scripting others. He summons them to say certain things, or act in certain ways.

Here his ambition seems like that of the most ambitious screenwriter. He wants to script 'the whole earth'. All lands and all nations are to sing the glory of God's name and to sing his praise. They are to say to God, 'How awesome are all your deeds!' (v.2). It is as though he can already see the scene he wants in his mind's eye, and envisages a limitless budget, with all the extras at his disposal that anyone could imagine.

But what is the real nature of this scripting? It might seem that it will involve the coercion of those who have no choice (like desperate wannabe actors who need the money). But the opening call – 'be joyful!' – doesn't mean 'act as though you are joyful!'. It really means what it says: '*be* joyful!'. This call is made not to create a glorious illusion of togetherness and fulfilment; it is based on the personal suffering and discovery that has convinced the psalmist where true joy is to be found. The scene he sees in his mind's eye is a vision of the hope and liberation of humanity, and his belief in its final necessity (rather than his desire for its artificial staging) is what makes him begin preparing (and auditioning) for it.

Reflection by **Ben Quash**

Refrain: *All the earth shall worship you, O Lord.*

Prayer: *How generous is your goodness, O God,*
how great is your salvation,
how faithful is your love;
help us to trust you in trial
and praise you in deliverance;
through Jesus Christ our Lord.

PSALM 66

Psalm 67

**God be gracious to us and bless us
and make his face to shine upon us.**

'God will bless us' (v.7)

This psalm expands and explains, democratizes and universalizes Aaron's ancient blessing (Numbers 6.24-26).

The peace and well-being that flow from the face of God are to be invoked not only by the priests in the Temple but by the whole congregation of worshippers wherever they meet. The gracious dealings of God are to be called upon not for Israel alone but for 'all the peoples of the world'.

The blessing that God gives to the nations is nothing less than God's 'saving power' (v.2), for God decides – or judges – for the peoples 'righteously' (v.4). The governance of God leads to the increase of the earth. It is an abundant blessing of abundance for the earth and it brings an abundance of joy.

Such joy cannot be silent. It produces praise. As the peoples are blessed by the goodness and graciousness of God, so they bless God, rejoicing in God's works and living in God's ways.

As the people of God at worship, we have a priestly vocation and a prophetic task. We are to call on God's blessing to be known among all the nations and we are to show what it is like to be a people who live under that blessing: a people who have seen the light of God, a people who have been shaped by the love of God, a people who have been set free to live for the praise of God.

Reflection by **Christopher Cocksworth**

Refrain: *Let the peoples praise you, O God;
let all the peoples praise you.*

Prayer: *In the face of Jesus Christ
your light and glory have blazed forth,
O God of all the nations;
with all your people,
may we make known your grace
and walk in the ways of peace;
for your name's sake.*

**Let God arise and let his enemies be scattered;
let those that hate him flee before him.**

'God gives the solitary a home' (v.6)

Scholars find this one of the most difficult psalms to understand, many concluding that it is a collection of Hebrew poetic fragments rather than an original unified work. The opening words of 'let God arise' appear to be a quotation from the book of Numbers (10.35) and this, with later references to 'solemn processions' (v.23), make some believe that the psalm was sung during an Autumn Festival procession of the Ark of the Covenant.

One of the obvious themes in the first half of the psalm is that of God being a shelter to those on the edges of an established society – the fatherless, widows, the solitary, prisoners, the poor and the weary. God's 'enemies' (v.1) are therefore those who ignore or abuse these groups that are dear to him. These enemies today will not always be individuals but structures and policies that grind the vulnerable down rather than protect them and work to meet their needs.

To place this conviction that God upholds those who suffer unfairness within a psalm that celebrates the movement of God, in liturgical procession and in human history, adds a focused momentum to the poem. It calls on those who pray these words as they journey 'to be saved from that patience that makes us patient with anything less than freedom and justice' (Martin Luther King Jr).

Reflection by **Mark Oakley**

Refrain: *Sing to God, sing praises to his name.*

Prayer: *Blessed are you, gracious God;*
you make your home among the weak,
you deliver us from death,
you bring us joy beyond our imagining
to the praise of Jesus Christ our Lord.

PSALM 68

Psalm 68, vv.18-end

Blessed be the Lord who bears our burdens day by day, for God is our salvation.

'... make music in praise of the Lord' (v.32)

Christian faith teaches us that God has given each of us a gift: it is called our *being*. The gift we are asked to give back in return is our *becoming*: the person we become as the years pass. We are all works in progress, but strangely tend to think that we're somehow complete. Not so – the person I am today is as transient as all the people I've ever been. The one constant is God. As we try to make our lives music in praise of this faithful and consistent God, played with increasing harmony and creativity, we realize that he is the 'cantus firmus', the fixed melody around which our own lives must shape themselves.

This psalm celebrates the music, movement and deliverance of a life lived with God. It celebrates the fact that it is God, not ourselves, who is our salvation (v.18) and that it is God who reaches out to us to touch us back into life. All we can do in response is bring gifts (v.28), sing to God (v.32) and ascribe power to him (v.34).

All that hinders or paralyses the music of our becoming is deathly and must be confronted for what it is. The author particularly names the 'lust after silver' and 'delight in war' (v.30). The desire to possess and compete can undo us rather than make us a more authentic gift to God. The poet ends with the words that express faith's beginning and end: 'Blessed be God'.

Reflection by **Mark Oakley**

Refrain: *Sing to God, sing praises to his name.*

Prayer: *Blessed are you, gracious God;*
you make your home among the weak,
you deliver us from death,
you bring us joy beyond our imagining
to the praise of Jesus Christ our Lord.

PSALM 68

Save me, O God,
for the waters have come up, even to my neck.

'You know my reproach, my shame and my dishonour' (v.21)

'I'm up to my neck in it!' – a phrase still used today even by people who don't know its origin here. But up to our neck in what?

Here 'it' is what the psalmist calls 'shame and reproach'. We have different names for it now, but most Christians have felt the effects of the culture of contempt: the constant mockery in the media; the unquestioned assumption that even the most intelligent Christian spokespeople are somehow bigoted or ignorant; even the way in which 'Christian' characters in soaps are usually portrayed as cranky or hypocritical. What makes it harder to deal with is that most Christians, just by virtue of being Christians, are already aware of their own failings. As the psalmist says, 'O God you know my foolishness, and my faults are not hidden from you' (v.6), and so we have to distinguish between the things for which we should be sorry, and the general 'shame' that is heaped on us for bearing witness to Christ – something that should count as a badge of honour.

This psalm helps with both. It confesses real faults, but also notes that we are blamed for virtue, that even humility is made a reproach. Thank God our Saviour knows the difference, that he knew the pain of false blame, that now he bears it in us and for us. It is small wonder that, after Psalm 22, this is the psalm that is most frequently quoted in the New Testament.

Reflection by **Malcolm Guite**

Refrain: *Hide not your face from your servant, O Lord.*

Prayer: *Thirsting on the cross,*
your Son shared the reproach of the oppressed
and carried the sins of all;
in him, O God, may the despairing find you,
the afflicted gain life
and the whole creation know its true king,
Jesus Christ our Lord.

PSALM 69

Psalm 69, vv.24-end

**Let the table before them be a trap
and their sacred feasts a snare.**

'I will praise the name of God with a song' (v.32)

Now here is some serious cursing: blindness, trembling in the loins, desolation, and finally complete erasure from the book of life!

If we are to understand the dark vehemence of this passage, we must look back to what became of the speaker at the end of yesterday's reading: 'Reproach has broken my heart ... They gave me gall to eat ... vinegar to drink' (vv.22-23). If we utterly crush someone, if we treat them so inhumanely that their humanity is destroyed, then we must expect from them only an inhuman response, as we are learning bitterly in the Middle East.

These cursing verses take us inside the heart of that hatred and violence that is itself the natural response to hatred and violence. They might seem therefore to offer no hope, no release from the cycle of violence, and yet somehow, shining through the cracks in its dark matter, this psalm offers a glimpse of a new song. The natural cycle of violence must somewhere be broken by something greater than nature. When this psalm finds its fulfilment in the New Testament, when Christ drinks the vinegar, and his broken heart is pierced, then what he says, is not the natural script of these cursing verses, but 'Father, forgive them' (Luke 23.34).

Reflection by **Malcolm Guite**

Refrain: *Hide not your face from your servant, O Lord.*

Prayer: *Thirsting on the cross,*
your Son shared the reproach of the oppressed
and carried the sins of all;
in him, O God, may the despairing find you,
the afflicted gain life
and the whole creation know its true king,
Jesus Christ our Lord.

O God, make speed to save me;
O Lord, make haste to help me.

'You are my help and my deliverer' (v.6)

This psalm is a real cry from the heart – a meditation on the feeling that our life is exposed and threatened. Those in this turmoil suffer a sense of helpless fear and suspicion.

Whether at school, at work, at a party, if you feel excluded, it hurts. We start imagining that people are talking unkindly about us. The psalmist's reference to those who laugh us to scorn seems all too real, though our suspicions may be baseless.

Of course, sometimes there *is* opposition – people really may wish us harm. Then it is fine to pray, with this psalmist, that their efforts will come to shame and confusion.

The good news is that we can replace our fear with praise! If we seek God with all our heart, we find ourselves rejoicing, and celebrating the greatness of God. God is our protector and hears us when we call on him.

Whatever life brings, crying out to God in the dark times will help us say, 'I will go on in the strength of the Lord'. Very much like the young men in the Book of Daniel: 'If our God whom we serve is able to deliver us from the furnace of blazing fire and out of your hand, O king, let him deliver us. But if not, be it known to you, O king, that we will not serve your gods and we will not worship the golden statue that you have set up.' (Daniel 3.17-18).

Sometimes God's timing seems too slow for us. That's when we just have to hang on in faith, hope and love.

Reflection by **John Sentamu**

Refrain: *Come to me quickly, O God.*

Prayer: *O God, our helper and defender,*
deliver us in our weakness,
answer our longings
and vindicate our faith,
that we may see your glory
in Jesus Christ our Lord.

PSALM 70

Psalm 71

In you, O Lord, do I seek refuge;
let me never be put to shame.

'... for I know no end of the telling' (v.15)

From the confidence of our youth to the trembling plea that God will not forsake us when our hair has turned grey, the prayer of this psalm seems to be that we will always remember to sing, even when our voices have become frail. We will sing not only with our lips and tongue but also with our soul, and as we ourselves move closer to the day when the deep earth will claim us, God's promise (v.20) is that we will be brought from the depths of the earth again.

The teaching of this song is a lesson we instinctively know: that the troubles and adversities we face as human beings are best seen with the hindsight of old age. Looking back, we can see patterns that emerge, and here the task given to those who are older is to show to the younger generation, by their words and their lives, the goodness and presence of God (vv.15-18).

This psalm gives clear purpose to living a long time: that the learning from experience is passed on to the next generation, and that greater age gives that task more weight and meaning. All that the older person asks is not to be forsaken by God, which is the same prayer prayed by old and young alike: that God will not leave.

Reflection by **Lucy Winkett**

Refrain: *O God, be not far from me.*

Prayer: *Faithful Lord, living Saviour,*
in youth and old age,
from the womb to the grave,
may we know your protection
and proclaim your great salvation
to the glory of God the Father.

Psalm 72

**Give the king your judgements, O God,
and your righteousness to the son of a king.**

'... have pity on the weak and poor' (v.13)

This psalm was written for King Solomon. It alludes to his name, which sounds a bit like *shalom*, the Hebrew word for peace and prosperity (v.3). It spells out things to pray for in a national leader. She or he should be just in creating the nation's legal policies (as the judge, v.2), economic policies (treating the poor with justice, v.2), social and health policies (on behalf of 'the children of the needy', v.4) and defence policies (when it is time to 'crush the oppressor', v.4). In fact, within the first four verses the psalm sets a compelling agenda for any government.

So how were these prayers for Solomon answered? Wisdom was a feature that characterized his reign. He gave the poor access to law courts, instituted international trade, built the Temple and (relatively, at least) secured peace. However, he also had a palace built for himself with slave labour, accumulated a vast personal fortune and dallied with the worship of idols. Unsurprisingly, he did not live forever (v.5). He laid the foundations of a national catastrophe that followed his death.

However, this psalm later came to be seen as a vision of the Messiah anticipated by the Jews. It is easy to recognize Jesus in these verses. He is eternal, righteous and ultimately triumphant in a way that no human could ever be. In him we truly have a leader who is 'established as long as the sun endures' (v.17).

Reflection by **Peter Graystone**

Refrain: *The Lord is king; let the earth rejoice.*

Prayer: *May your kingdom come, O God,
with deliverance for the needy,
with peace for the righteous,
with overflowing blessing for all nations,
with glory, honour and praise
for Christ, the only Saviour.*

PSALM 72

Psalm 73

**Truly, God is loving to Israel,
to those who are pure in heart.**

'I was but foolish and ignorant' (v.22)

We can set our compass on God's way, and we can wander from it. We can also stumble.

Psalm 73 is one of the most human of the psalms. The psalmist begins by asserting the benevolence of God, but then, like Peter, almost overwhelmed when he notices the waves (Matthew 14.30), his faith starts to wobble. He looks around and draws acute observations about the lives of those who do not trust God. Not only do they prosper materially, they are admired by others and fêted as the leaders of society.

The psalmist honestly asks himself if the demanding way he has been walking is actually worth it, and in verse 15 there is an indication that he may have been tempted to abandon it for an easier life. Perhaps this is a psalm that helped Jesus during his own temptation.

This dilemma is beyond human understanding, but the psalmist does something wise. He intentionally places himself in a position from which he may best glimpse the divine perspective. (Jesus talks of the divine perspective as something that can be lost through a 'stumbling-block' in Matthew 16.23.) For the psalmist, this is to go to his place of worship. Here he sees that his preoccupation with the lives of others has diverted him from a fundamental truth: like Peter trying to walk on the water, God is with the psalmist, holding him to comfort, lift and lead on the right path. So is he with us.

Reflection by **Joanna Collicutt**

PSALM 73

Refrain: *In the Lord God have I made my refuge.*

Prayer: *Holy God,
may we find wisdom in your presence
and set our hope not on uncertain riches
but on the love that holds us to the end;
in Jesus Christ our Lord.*

O God, why have you utterly disowned us?
Why does your anger burn against the sheep of your pasture?

'... who did deeds of salvation in the midst of the earth' (v.11)

If you were asked to describe God, I wonder what you might say? Within the Christian tradition we often attribute abstract qualities to God – God is love, patient and kind, just and righteous. These are all good and accurate descriptions of God, but they only take us so far in our understanding of who God is.

It is interesting to notice that in the Old Testament, and particularly in the Psalms, when they wanted to talk about God, they told and retold the stories about what he had done. Psalm 74 is a particularly good example of this. Something disastrous has clearly befallen the nation (vv.1-11), and the people are bewildered and in chaos. In response to this, the psalmist recalls what God has done in performing 'deeds of salvation in the midst of the earth' (v.11).

You may notice that the psalmist does not keep to the strict chronology of the story (vv.12-17); he draws in references to creation, to the exodus and to the wilderness wanderings in a reminder of who God is. Part of this story involves the crushing of Leviathian, a great sea-monster referred to a few times in the Psalms, in Job and in Isaiah that stands as a symbol of chaos and rebellion against God. How do we know how God will act? Because this is what he did time and time again. What God did is who God is, and this offers us comfort in the chaos.

Reflection by **Paula Gooder**

Refrain: *Arise, O God, maintain your own cause.*

Prayer: *Redeeming God,*
renew your broken people
with your Holy Spirit,
that they may walk your narrow way,
and greet your coming dawn
in Jesus Christ our Lord.

PSALM 74

Psalm 75

**We give you thanks, O God, we give you thanks,
for your name is near, as your wonderful deeds declare.**

'It is I that hold her pillars steady' (v.3)

There is a conversation going on. It is difficult to tell who is speaking when, but it seems that God speaks first, and in response the psalmist affirms what God has said. The theme is God's power over the world.

The psalm's imagery shows us a fragile and damaged world. Its very foundations are shaken by the actions of marauding nations. Their armies rampage around the earth with such force that it is like a rhinoceros going full tilt at the walls of a house. God's people look to the east and west, and to the southern deserts, hoping for rescue, but none comes.

But the psalmist speaks with confidence. The earth will not break apart, because God is holding it together. At the heart of the world is a strong, steady presence. And that presence never stays still for long; soon it will be on the move. The weapons that have caused so much damage will be broken, and God's judgement cup will incapacitate armies. The world will be stabilized.

When our world seems to rock on its foundations, we have hope. It was God who created it, and it is God who holds it steady until his purposes for it can be fulfilled. We can share the confidence of the psalmist, and say, 'I will rejoice for ever, and make music to the God of Jacob' (v.10).

Reflection by **Gillian Cooper**

Refrain: *God alone is judge.*

Prayer: *Judge of all the earth,
restrain the ambition of the proud
and establish among us the reign of the Messiah,
who drained for us the cup of judgement
and is alive with you and the Holy Spirit,
one God, for ever and ever.*

In Judah God is known;
his name is great in Israel.

'But you indeed are awesome!' (v.7, NRSV)

According to the American writer, Anne Lamott, the prayer of the Daily Offices can be simply summarised. Morning Prayer can be condensed into a single word: 'Whatever'. And Evening Prayer needs only two words: 'Ah, well...'. Lamott says elsewhere there are really only three other prayers: 'Help', 'Thanks' and 'Wow!'. We perhaps spend too much time asking, she suggests – pleading, really – and not enough thanking. And very little time just saying of and to God, 'Wow!'.

Prayer is one of those activities that Christians (indeed, folk of all faiths) engage in, but seldom pause to consider what it is they are doing. The habitual, impromptu and mysterious nature of prayer is part of its fascination. Here we have the language of faith, of desire, of hope, of healing – and even occasionally of justification and commination (threatening sinners with divine judgement). And occasionally the quirky: 'Hail, Mary, full of grace, help me find a parking space' – a prayer that not only rhymes, but also seems to work – for some.

The psalmist here uses words and ideas that might belong more easily to the vocabulary of younger readers – 'Wow!' and 'Awesome!' come to mind. The psalmist has been struck by the majesty, grandeur and power of God. There are few words or syllables that will do God justice here. Before the word of God, all are reduced to stupefied silence; we are dumb before the God who speaks. Before the face of God, don't feel the need to babble on; less is more. 'Wow!' and 'Awesome!' as exclamations of praise will do fine.

Reflection by **Martyn Percy**

Refrain: *The Lord has made fast his throne for judgement.*

Prayer: *Majestic and gracious God,*
more awesome than the agents of war,
more powerful than the wrath of nations,
restrain the violence of the peoples
and draw the despised of the earth
into the joyful life of your kingdom,
where you live and reign for ever and ever.

PSALM 76

Psalm 77

I cry aloud to God;
I cry aloud to God and he will hear me.

'I will remember the works of the Lord' (v. 11)

Remembering is at the centre of this psalm. The main Hebrew verb for it occurs four times, though English versions tend to use different words to translate it. On three of these occasions (vv.3,6,11), it stands at the beginning of the verse. The fourth is when it is repeated in the second half of verse 11. Given the norm in Hebrew poetry of varying terms between the two halves of the verse, it is hard to imagine a more vivid way of drawing our attention to the centrality of remembering in this psalm, at its pivotal point.

And it does pivot between verses 10 and 11: something changes in that short space between them. In the first part, the psalmist remembers – and is brought low. In the second part, the psalmist remembers – and is lifted up. What has happened?

In the second part, remembrance is located in address to God, not circling thoughts about God: rather than remembering 'the days of old', the psalmist remembers 'your wonders of old time' (v.11). Address leads to adoration – 'Your way, O God, is holy' (v.13). Adoration opens the imagination to enter anew into the work of God, the spirit to see with the eyes of the faithful from every age, and the mind to name the threads of divine faithfulness that weave past and present into one. 'You led your people like sheep by the hand of Moses and Aaron' (v.20). We have passed over.

Reflection by **Jeremy Worthen**

Refrain: *In the day of my trouble I have sought the Lord.*

Prayer: *God our shepherd,*
you led us and saved us in times of old;
do not forget your people in their troubles,
but raise up your power
to sustain the poor and helpless;
for the honour of Jesus Christ our Lord.

**Hear my teaching, O my people;
incline your ears to the words of my mouth.**

'So that they might put their trust in God' (v.7)

Psalm 78 is a long narrative of the history of the people of Israel from their early days as they were led out of bondage in Egypt until the reign of King David. It is a story told with the purpose of encouraging the coming generations to be faithful to God and to trust him.

The psychosocial significance of narratives is becoming increasingly understood. They are a way that we construct our identity, both as individuals and communities, and if we lose them, we are in danger of losing ourselves. They express our values, and are one important way in which we make sense of our lives – weaving what might be a series of random events into a cohesive script. Older generations often express a need to pass on wisdom to the next, and the main way they do this is in telling a story. It has been noted that human beings have a tendency to tell 'redemptive' narratives; we have an instinct to make good rather than bad meaning.

So this psalm can be read as the story of God's people, into which are woven the key events of their past in such a way as to draw meaning from them, and to assert that the Lord is not some sort of capricious despot, but a God who orders his relationship with his people according to certain rules. The psalmist is essentially asserting that things happen for a purpose, or in more contemporary language, 'The universe is on your side – even if it doesn't always feel like it.'

Reflection by **Joanna Collicutt**

Refrain: *O Lord, how glorious are your works.*

Prayer: *God our deliverer,
as you led our ancestors through the wilderness,
so lead us through the wilderness of this world,
that we may be saved through Christ for ever.*

PSALM 78

103

Psalm 78, vv.40-end

How often they rebelled against him in the wilderness and grieved him in the desert!

'With skilful hands he guided them' (v.72)

The story has a very long time span, covering hundreds of years. It asserts the power and sovereignty of God, and his starting position of love for his people, through which he saved them from the waters of the Red Sea and led them through the wilderness (vv.51-53), providing food and drink, and eventually a permanent secure home.

This is a picture of the overflowing grace of a God who gives in abundance (vv.20,24). It is also a picture of a people who do not appreciate God's generosity but take both his gifts and his merciful forgiveness for granted (see also Romans 2.4). Out of this develops something worse: a sense of entitlement.

All of this seems to stem from the people forgetting their own story. Again and again the psalmist exhorts his listeners to remember. There are some things that should not be forgotten. Where there is national freedom and prosperity, it has usually been hard won by previous generations, and maintained by the continuing sacrifices of many. Their stories must be heard and remembered: that is why civic acts of memorial are so central to the identity of a country.

So also would we do well to examine our hearts for a casual attitude to God and a grasping at the things of this world. And lest we forget, we have the story of Jesus that gives us our identity: 'who, though he was in the form of God, did not regard equality with God a thing to be grasped but ... became obedient unto death' (Philippians 2.6,8 (RSV)).

Reflection by **Joanna Collicutt**

Refrain: *Tremble, O earth, at the presence of the Lord.*

Prayer: *God our shepherd,*
in all our wanderings and temptations,
teach us to rest in your mercy
and trust in your defence;
through him who laid down his life for us,
Jesus Christ our Lord.

**O God, the heathen have come into your heritage;
your holy temple have they defiled
and made Jerusalem a heap of stones.**

*'Let your compassion make haste to meet us,
for we are brought very low' (v.8)*

How will it be when we are tested by disaster? This psalm records the almost unimaginable horror of the temple overthrown, its hallows defiled, innocent people butchered, blood flowing in the streets, unburied corpses everywhere. It happened to Jerusalem in 587 BC and again in AD 70, and this psalm was recited on the anniversaries of both disasters.

Of course there is a call for revenge – it wouldn't be an honest poem if there wasn't – and yet, as always in the mystery of the psalms, there is something more. We have vengeance in verse 6 but compassion in verse 8, even if it is only compassion for Israel. There is a confession in verse 9 that 'we' are not without fault, and by verse 12 we have a beautiful prayer that is at least capable of including not only those led off captive to Babylon, but every prisoner everywhere, a prayer that many of us may pray today for those in our own prisons.

If the worst happens and we have a 'major incident', a terrorist attack in our capital, there will be lamentation, there will be voices crying for vengeance, but will we also find in our hearts – and give voice to – both the confession and the compassion that are threaded so strangely through this despairing psalm?

Reflection by **Malcolm Guite**

Refrain: *Help us, O God of our salvation, for the glory
of your name.*

Prayer: *When faith is scorned
and love grows cold,
then, God of hosts, rebuild your Church
on lives of thankfulness and patient prayer;
through Christ your eternal Son.*

PSALM 79

Psalm 80

**Hear, O Shepherd of Israel,
you that led Joseph like a flock.**

'Cherish this vine which your right hand has planted' (v.16)

Christian tradition speaks of the Psalms as a mirror, in which we can see reflected what Athanasius of Alexandria, writing in the fourth century, called 'the movements of the soul'. Yet this is a paradoxical mirror, in that beholding our reflection here also changes us, drawing us into the likeness of Christ, our true identity.

What are we asking for when we pray with the psalmist, 'show the light of your countenance, and we shall be saved' (vv.4,8,20)? At different times, different things will be at the forefront of our minds, just as at different periods of biblical history, those who prayed this psalm had varying concerns. There is space here for all manner of cries from the human heart.

Yet wherever we may begin in our pleas to God today, the psalm does not leave us there. In verse 9, the perspective apparently switches: we are no longer speaking of ourselves and our present troubles, but of a vine, an image that embraces centuries of history and sketches an intimate relationship between God and God's people. What matters is not so much our suffering in isolation but the fracturing of that relationship. What matters is the vine, which is God's people across the generations and also somehow one person, 'the son of man you have made so strong for yourself' (v.18). We know that our restoration, our illumination, our salvation depend on this vine. Therefore we cry out in security as well as in longing, for however bruised it may be, God will never forsake it.

Reflection by **Jeremy Worthen**

Refrain: *Turn us again, O God;
show the light of your countenance, and we shall
be saved.*

Prayer: *Faithful shepherd of your people,
as we look for the light of your countenance,
restore in us the image of your glory
and graft us into the risen life of your Son,
Jesus Christ our Lord.*

**Sing merrily to God our strength,
shout for joy to the God of Jacob.**

'... honey from the rock' (v.16)

The Psalms are full of musical instruments that might conjure up for us a picture of renaissance angels diving between the clouds plucking their harps as they go. For some, this music making is evocative of the presence of God; for others, it is alienating. But the music doesn't have to be so literal as to invoke memories of perhaps painful school choir practices.

The Hebrew word *tehila*, from which we get *tehillim*, the Hebrew name for the Psalms, means both 'praise' and a piece of music. We also get the acclamation 'halleluya' from this root. So the praise of God, the affirmation of the glory of God, is itself a form of music, a higher expression of our instinct to worship God beyond us, however good or bad we think we are at actual singing. In this context, this psalm of praise is an eruption of thankfulness poured into a natural world that is already singing and full of praise (music). The cycles of the moon mark the passing of time (v.3), and our praise is constant throughout, ready to start again when the moon is new again.

Whatever our circumstances, in slavery or freedom (v.5), even when we don't recognize the voice or presence of God (vv.6ff.), our shouts and songs are asked of us, in the knowledge that everything we have and all that we are find their origin and purpose in God.

Reflection by **Lucy Winkett**

Refrain: *O come, let us sing to the Lord.*

Prayer: *Father of mercy,
keep us joyful in your salvation
and faithful to your covenant;
and, as we journey to your kingdom,
ever feed us with the bread of life,
your Son, our Saviour Jesus Christ.*

Psalm 82

**God has taken his stand in the council of heaven;
in the midst of the gods he gives judgement.**

*'Rescue the weak and the poor;
deliver them from the hand of the wicked' (v.4)*

Jewish tradition (reflected in Jesus' words in John 10.34-36) interpreted this psalm as condemning the human rulers of Israel for acting unjustly and unfairly. Viewed in its historical context, however, the psalm reflects the belief that the God of Israel was one among many, and was undoubtedly the most powerful. The psalmist, through the use of the imagery of a council, is attempting to persuade others of the greatness of God. Other gods are portrayed as being insignificant and incompetent beings.

Although the imagery of judgement lends itself to a reflection of power, the deeper aspect of this arena of metaphor is in fact that of ethics. God as judge is infinitely more ethical than his counterparts, and that alone sets God apart.

There is a rich heritage to the prioritizing of the last, lost and least in the Judaeo-Christian tradition. Though God is omnipotent, that power is exercised for the benefit of those who are most vulnerable. This is both a reminder and a challenge to us as we pray this psalm that the call of our faith upon our lives is to search for those who have no voice and who are marginalized for whatever reason. God is not God of the rich, but of the poor.

Reflection by **Helen-Ann Hartley**

PSALM 82

Refrain: *Arise, O God, and judge the earth.*

Prayer: *God our deliverer,
when the foundations are shaken
and justice has departed,
defend the poor and needy
and give your people strength to fight all wrong
in the name of your Son, Jesus Christ our Lord.*

**Hold not your peace, O God, do not keep silent;
be not unmoved, O God.**

*'O my God, make them like thistledown,
like chaff before the wind' (v.13)*

There aren't many places where we're allowed to express our darkest thoughts without restraint, and it may come as a surprise that praying with the Bible is one of them. The wonderful gift of the psalms is that all human life is here, including the powerful negative feelings we usually suppress for the greater good. Would we dare to copy satirical novelist Samuel Butler who said, 'It was very good of God to let Thomas and Mrs Carlyle marry one another and so make only two people miserable instead of four'? Similarly, the psalmist is nothing if not honest, exhorting God to 'O my God, make them like thistledown, like chaff before the wind', to 'drive them with your tempest and dismay them with your storm' (vv.13,15). Whatever happened to the Sermon on the Mount?

But that's just the point. The Bible takes us on a journey. It takes us from wherever we are, flying free as an eagle or stuck in quicksand, and leads us to a larger, wiser space. As is often said, God loves us just as we are, but loves us too much to let us stay that way. I value a sacred document that recognizes the heart of darkness within me but always wants something better. I don't propose to describe my demons in public, but each of us could benefit from owning the side of us hidden in shadow and then, having fully accepted its presence, set about exposing it to the light of Christ.

What is there that you might bring out of the cellar and let Christ love into life?

Reflection by **John Pritchard**

Refrain: *The wicked shall not be able to stand
in the judgement.*

Prayer: *Lord God, most high over all the world,
when the pride of nations obscures
your glorious purpose,
draw us into that unity which is your will for all people
in Jesus Christ our Lord.*

PSALM 83

Psalm 84

**How lovely is your dwelling place, O Lord of hosts!
My soul has a desire and longing to enter the courts
of the Lord.**

'For one day in your courts is better than a thousand' (v.9)

This psalm is often referred to as a pilgrim psalm. Here the writer is joyfully looking forward to arriving in the holy place of God. The sense of anticipation of entering the temple is clear, and the whole psalm is bound together by addressing God as 'Lord of hosts', and with an exhilarating sense of praise.

This is perhaps a welcome interlude in the midst of psalms of lament, and yet another reminder that lament is always balanced by praise. Sadness is always accompanied by hope and joy. Those who live in God's temple are pleased to be there, as well as those who are making a pilgrimage in that direction. God is praised as the one providing protection, both as a bird nesting her young (one of many examples of feminine imagery for God), and as a shield from the glare of the sun.

That God too is the source of the energy and power means that God is acknowledged as present and involved in every aspect of life. Beyond the scope of the temporal relief from oppression and extremes of weather, God's scope reaches into eternity. This psalm acknowledges the distant reaches of God's care, with one day in his presence more prized than a thousand. There is much to be gained from such perspective.

Reflection by **Helen-Ann Hartley**

Refrain: *Blessed are they who dwell in your house.*

Prayer: *Lord God,
sustain us in this vale of tears
with the vision of your grace and glory,
that, strengthened by the bread of life,
we may come to your eternal dwelling place;
in the power of Jesus Christ our Lord.*

PSALM 84

**Lord, you were gracious to your land;
you restored the fortunes of Jacob.**

'... righteousness and peace have kissed' (v.10)

Dream on. The kind of hopeful, just and peaceful world for which we long can seem like a dream ... a foolish, receding dream likely only to encounter the ironic response, 'Dream on!' – an invitation to stop dreaming.

This psalm dreams of restoration of fortune to the psalmist's community. It comes to the conclusion that good fortune and prosperity will only come to a people who are themselves just, peaceable and peaceful. For the psalmist this dream of prosperity and peace is born out of the memory of previous restorations. God, you restored us before, spoke peace to us before – please do the same again. And however unlikely this may seem to us right now, in God's grace people *have* learned, at certain times and in certain places, to live in love and peace with all. So is the dream so foolish after all?

The seed of peace is God's. But so much of the nurturing of that seed is down to us where we are. The path to a more peaceful world must begin to take shape in *our* hearts, on *our* lips and through *our* hands. Peace must start here, with you and with me.

The psalmist uses the beautiful image of the kiss to shape the conclusion to this psalm. When righteousness and peace kiss – when they embrace in and through us – goodness will ripple out into the world. So dream on – hope, pray and act. Dream on.

Reflection by **Ian Adams**

Refrain: *Show us your mercy, O Lord.*

Prayer: *Most holy God,
when we come to you fearing that
    truth condemns us,
show us that truth is one with love
in your Word made flesh,
our Saviour Jesus Christ.*

PSALM 85

Psalm 86

**Incline your ear, O Lord, and answer me,
for I am poor and in misery.**

'In the day of my distress' (v.7)

In this psalm we encounter one of the truly great gifts of the psalms: the space they give to darkness, loss and distress. This space rarely comes with easy answers but only with some long-accumulated sense of God's goodness to give us any hope at all. Whatever the circumstances of our own despair, the psalm-community, it seems, has been here many times before us and will always return to share with us grounds for some quiet hope within our darkness.

This particular psalm represents a headlong dive into the compassionate character of God, becoming a meditation on God's consistent love and mercy. Here the psalm reflects a common contemplative experience in the Judaeo-Christian tradition, voicing a desire for union with God – 'knit my heart to you' (v.11). In the darkness God's love is eliciting love from the psalmist – and from us. Love calls love.

But the psalm ends in a desperate call for a sign, a token of God's love. Any hint of light will do! This of course is how life and prayer often turn out. It can feel as if there's a gap between concept and reality. Distress hangs around. Darkness persists. Any light remains faint on the far horizon. Perhaps, in the spirit of this psalm – and in the tradition's memory of God's love and mercy – we need to learn the art of being at the same time both *in darkness* and *in love*

Reflection by **Ian Adams**

Refrain: *All nations you have made shall come and worship you, O Lord.*

Prayer: *God of mercy,
who in your great love
drew your Son from the depths of the Pit,
bring your people from death to life,
that we may rejoice in your compassion
and praise you now and for ever.*

His foundation is on the holy mountains.
The Lord loves the gates of Zion
more than all the dwellings of Jacob.

'This one also was born there' (v. 5)

This is a psalm of universal promise. The theme of God's choice of Mount Zion as the dwelling place for his name is familiar in many of the psalms. But in this psalm it is made clear that this does not mean that God's love is reserved only for those who are linked to Jerusalem by living in the land of Israel. The psalmist unveils a miracle, announcing that Zion is in fact the secret birthplace of all those who love God whatever their background, faith, ethnicity or nationality. God names and recognizes everyone and enrols them in his eternal purpose. Even Israel's most formidable enemies, Egypt and Babylon, are counted among those who know God, who are included in his promise.

This is a psalm to pray with when we want to give thanks for the grace and mercy of God or in times of doubt and distress when we wonder whether our faith and commitment really mean anything. The source of our hope does not lie in ourselves but in that miracle by which God counts us as his own. For those who dare to believe, the fresh springs of the water of life never run dry. We are born for joy, for the singing and dancing prophesied here, not for despair.

Reflection by **Angela Tilby**

Refrain: *The Lord has chosen Zion for himself.*

Prayer: *Lord, as you call us to your city*
founded on the rock of ages,
let the springs of living water
rise within us to eternal life;
in Jesus Christ our Lord.

PSALM 87

Psalm 88

O Lord, God of my salvation,
I have cried day and night before you.

'For my soul is full of troubles' (v.3)

Psalm 88 is the most unusual of all the lament psalms. Psalms of lament in the Psalter have all got one thing in common: no matter how bleak the psalmist's outlook, they always end in praise and a statement of confidence in who God is, and all that he has done and will continue to do. The exception is this psalm.

Psalm 88 is bleak from beginning to end – it begins with describing how full of troubles the psalmist's life is and ends with a statement declaring the extent of God's wrath against him. In this one psalm out of the whole Psalter there is no let up, no relief and no hope.

This psalm arose out of and speaks into unremitting gloom. Many of us, at some point in our life, will sink into a pit of emotional gloom as deep and hopeless as the one that gave rise to this psalm. Those who have been there will tell you that in the midst of despair, try as we might, we simply cannot remember who God is, let alone recount his mighty deeds of salvation. This psalmist appears to understands this and offers us a different way forward: to address our grief, our hopelessness and despair to God.

It provides no easy way out, no simple solutions but does remind us that, no matter what we feel like, God will hear our cry.

Reflection by **Paula Gooder**

Refrain: *You are my refuge, my portion in the land of the living.*

Prayer: *In the depths of our isolation*
we cry to you, Lord God;
give light in our darkness
and bring us out of the prison of our despair
through Jesus Christ our Lord.

**My song shall be always of the loving-kindness of the Lord:
with my mouth will I proclaim your faithfulness
throughout all generations.**

'Strong is your hand' (v.13)

This long psalm is an extraordinary example of honest, fierce, intercessory prayer. Thirty-seven verses of descriptive praise lead up to a 'but' that offers a challenge to God. Although we read it in its three separate parts, reading through the whole psalm at once gives us a sense of how clever and daring this prayer really is.

We begin with a statement that will prove crucial later: God has made a covenant with King David and his successors that is 'firm as the heavens' (v.2). 'How firm is that?' the psalmist asks. The whole earth is securely under God's control. The chaos of the sea, represented by the monster Rahab, has been tamed and put in its place. God's rule extends north and south, east and west. And it is not just the earth that is under God's thumb. He rules over the heavenly beings too. His reign is characterized by righteousness and justice, by steadfast love and faithfulness.

So God's people can rest secure. The God who is their king is in absolute control. He has power over the universe, and has promised to keep them safe for all time. No wonder they rejoice all the day long.

The psalmist leaves us in no doubt. God has made an agreement that he is well able to keep. There is no limit to his power that would compromise his ability to deliver on his promises.

Reflection by **Gillian Cooper**

Refrain: *Truly the Lord is our shield.*

Prayer: *As we sing of your love, O Lord,*
anoint us with the Spirit's seal,
that we may praise your faithfulness
and proclaim your truth from age to age;
through Jesus Christ our Lord.

PSALM 89

Psalm 89, vv.19-37

You spoke once in a vision and said to your faithful people:
'I have set a youth above the mighty;
I have raised a young man over the people...'

'I will not take from him my steadfast love' (v.33)

The key term in this section of the psalm is 'steadfast love', *hesed* in Hebrew. The word is difficult to translate into English. It has nothing to do with emotion, and everything to do with an act of will. It means strong, faithful commitment. Here the psalmist reminds God that *hesed* is what God promised David and his successors. Even if they went astray, his *hesed* would not fail, but would last for ever. There would be a king on the throne of David as long as the sun and moon appeared in the sky, and the king would have God's protection from his enemies because he would continue to be God's anointed one, his son. The language echoes that of the story of God's promises to David told in 2 Samuel 7.

The covenant between God and David is hugely important in much of the Old Testament. It is what shapes the life of Israel before the Exile, and what causes such a crisis of faith when it fails that the whole relationship between God and his people has to be completely re-thought. There are various Old Testament 'covenants', forms of agreement between God and his people, but the key to this covenant is that it cannot be broken, no matter what. That is what the psalmist wants us to know beyond any doubt, before we move on to the end of his prayer.

Reflection by **Gillian Cooper**

PSALM 89

Refrain: *The Lord has sworn an oath to David,*
a promise from which he will not shrink.

Prayer: *Faithful God,*
remember your promise
fulfilled in your anointed Son Jesus Christ,
in whose strength alone we stand,
now and for ever.

**But you have cast off and rejected your anointed;
you have shown fierce anger against him.**

'You have broken the covenant' (v.39)

'But now,' says the Psalmist. It has taken 37 verses to reach that 'but', and now we see where it has all been leading. We, and God, have been given the context unequivocally. We know that God has made promises. We know that those promises are unconditional. We know that God's power to deliver is not limited. 'But now ....'

The covenant has been broken, and not by Israel. God has reneged on his promises. The king's reign lies in ruins with his palace.

So the psalmist justifiably calls God to account. 'Where, O Lord, is your steadfast love of old, which you swore to David in your faithfulness?' (v.49) Faithfulness was sworn and expected, but God has not delivered. He has acted against, rather than for, his covenant partner. The psalmist looks God in the eye and makes his bold accusation: your performance, Lord, is simply not good enough. It will not do. It has to change.

Verse 52 marks the end of this section of the book of Psalms, and is not, strictly speaking, part of this psalm. The psalm does not revert to praise. It ends with question and accusation. Of course we know that God's promises are always ultimately fulfilled, in ways the Psalmist cannot imagine. But in the middle of things, when our world is falling about our ears, the psalmist gives us words so that we do not turn our backs on God, but can honestly look God in the eye.

Reflection by **Gillian Cooper**

Refrain: *For your servant David's sake,*
turn not away the face of your anointed.

Prayer: *Lord, when death appals us*
and you hide your face,
may we know our life is hidden with Christ,
our hope of glory and our risen Lord.

PSALM 89

Psalm 90

**Lord, you have been our refuge
from one generation to another.**

'... from everlasting to everlasting you are God' (v.2)

We may well be able to identify with the writers of the Psalms; swept up on the roller-coaster that is life, experiencing to the greatest heights and lowest depths the triumphs and tragedies, the joys and sorrows of daily living. But the writer of Psalm 90 takes a different approach; his comments appear to arise from the wisdom of age and the standpoint of eternity: 'Lord, you have been our refuge from one generation to another' (v.1).

The canvas is vast, stretching from before the creation to the consummation of all things at the end of time: 'from everlasting to everlasting you are God' (v.2). And within this overarching scheme humanity takes its place, following the same arc from birth to death as the rest of creation. And all that humans achieve 'is but labour and sorrow, for they soon pass away and we are gone' (v.10).

Despite this apparent futility, however, there is hope and meaning. We see parallels with the book of Ecclesiastes, but here, as there, the psalmist's aim is to stimulate the search for wisdom. Despite the brevity of life, we are held by God in our living and our dying, and when we first seek his wisdom, we will know true joy and gladness (v.14).

Today, let us make the prayer of the psalmist our own: 'So teach us to number our days that we may apply our hearts to wisdom' (v.12).

Reflection by **Barbara Mosse**

PSALM 90

Refrain: *O Lord my God, in you I take refuge.*

Prayer: *Almighty God,
our eternal refuge,
teach us to live with the knowledge of our death
and to rejoice in the promise of your glory,
revealed to us in Jesus Christ our Lord.*

**Whoever dwells in the shelter of the Most High
and abides under the shadow of the Almighty...**

'You shall not be afraid' (v.5)

One of the most rich and beautiful poems in Scripture encourages us to trust ever more deeply in God, to the degree that we will be gently put back on our feet when we stumble over a rock (v.12). As elsewhere in the Psalms (e.g. 57, 61, 63), the wings of God guard us and it is under those wings that we live, with the unalterably gentle image of feathers, peaceful in themselves but deceptively strong against the wind and rain of the world.

But it is the teaching hidden in verse 6 that might strike a chord with contemporary life. The desert fathers and mothers of the fourth century meditated on the 'sickness that destroys at noonday' and called it *akedia*, or spiritual listlessness. This deep sense of futility, they suggested, strikes not in the dark night of despair but at noon, when the sun is high, when we are active and busy, when we are under the sun working, relating to others, getting on with things. Our busy-ness can become distraction from our deeper purposes, and our spirits become depressed, submerged under the bustle and preoccupations of our days.

We often concentrate on the tragedies of our lives when looking for explanations for our struggles in our spiritual lives, but this psalm teaches us that one of the more dangerous moments of our journey is when the sun is high and we are in the noonday of our lives – brightly lit, working hard, nowhere to hide.

Reflection by **Lucy Winkett**

Refrain: *Keep me as the apple of your eye.*

Prayer: *Keep us, good Lord,
under the shadow of your mercy
and, as you have bound us to yourself in love,
leave us not who call upon your name,
but grant us your salvation,
made known in the cross of Jesus Christ our Lord.*

PSALM 91

Psalm 92

**It is a good thing to give thanks to the Lord
and to sing praises to your name, O Most High.**

'... faithfulness in the night-time' (v.2)

This is a psalm of thanksgiving, and we know that it was originally used as part of worship on the Sabbath. As with most psalms of gratitude, it reminds us that it is good to sing. It also reminds us that we thank God because of the depths of his wisdom (v.5) and the ways in which his love carries us through a precarious life (v.4). Not to recognize these things, says the poet, would be to join the fools and wicked who are always around but invariably come to ruin (v.11).

Palms are luxuriant plants and Lebanon's cedars were renowned for being tall and strong. If planted well, they get the nutrients they need and are noticed for both their health and beauty. So it is, continues the psalmist, for the righteous who, planted in the divine presence, show in their integrated, thankful lives 'that the Lord is true' (v.15).

A line has always struck me in this psalm. Verse 2 says it is good to tell of God's faithfulness in the night-time. It has metaphoric resonance. Even when we are living through dark times, when we are restless and in need of peace, we learn in the painful silence that we don't always speak God's language and must become children again, re-created and shaped by a wisdom very distant from the world's outlook and given a body-language in the man of Nazareth.

Reflection by **Mark Oakley**

Refrain: *You, O Lord, shall be exalted for evermore.*

Prayer: *Give us the music of your praise, Lord,
morning, noon and night,
that our lives may be fruitful
and our lips confess you as the true and only God.*

**The Lord is king and has put on glorious apparel;
the Lord has put on his glory
and girded himself with strength.**

'Mightier than the thunder of many waters' (v.5)

This psalm is an enthronement psalm. Here God is lauded as a king in all his glory and finery. The psalm is intended to demonstrate that God is king, that his rule is stable and prosperous, everlasting and ultimately reliable. In the context of competing kingdoms and threats to divine order and power, the reiteration of such a psalm fostered a deep sense of the importance and longevity of God's rule.

But more than all that, God's power in creation and in order over chaos is also alluded to in this psalm, more reason to accede to his power and rule. Imagery of watery domains can be found littered throughout the biblical narrative. The first act of creation tells of the subduing of the waters, and throughout the Psalter, references to water are made as a way of heightening the importance and ability of God's rule.

There is something all encompassing about the scope of this psalm, which offers us an opportunity to look beyond ourselves. When you stand on the shoreline looking out to sea, you cannot see beyond the horizon. But we know and trust that what lies beyond our view is land beyond the sea. Even if that is far away, the scope of our world is bound by creative forces that tell of the glory of God.

Reflection by **Helen-Ann Hartley**

Refrain: The Lord shall reign for ever and ever.

Prayer: Christ our King,
you put on the apparel of our nature
and raised us to your glory;
reign from your royal throne
above the chaos of this world,
that all may see the victory you have won
and trust in your salvation;
for your glory's sake.

PSALM 93

Psalm 94

Lord God to whom vengeance belongs,
O God to whom vengeance belongs, shine out in majesty.

'Who will rise up for me against the wicked?' (v.16)

Psalm 94 is a liturgy for different voices, a play with different parts. The scene is set by the first chorus (vv.1-7), lamenting the state of the world and crying out to God to rise up and set things right.

The second chorus responds (vv.8-15) drawing on the language of assurance from the prophets (compare Isaiah 40.28 for tone). The turmoil in the world is no grounds for despair. Justice and righteousness will return.

But after this exchange a different voice breaks in. 'Who will rise up for me ...? Who will take my part...?' God speaks. Is this the voice heard by Isaiah in the worship of the temple: 'Whom shall I send, and who will go for us?' (Isaiah 6.8). God invites disciples to join this great mission to establish justice in the earth. God calls individuals to play their part.

We are meant to pause and hear the question before we attend to the answer. The questions should hang in the air for a moment, inviting us to answer.

Then, in the psalm, a solo voice responds – most probably the king in the ancient liturgy of the temple. The one called by God says yes to that call, in humility and trust. 'Here am I, send me!' (Isaiah 6.8).

Reflection by **Steven Croft**

Refrain: *Righteous are you, O Lord, and true are your judgements.*

Prayer: *Lord God, judge of all,*
before whom no secrets are hidden,
let your justice shine out
and your righteousness sweep wickedness from its throne,
that we may live free from fear and stumbling;
through Jesus Christ our Lord.

**O come, let us sing to the Lord;
let us heartily rejoice in the rock of our salvation.**

'Let us come into his presence with thanksgiving' (v.2)

A theme that runs through the whole Psalter is here made explicit: God reigns. This remains true whether the present circumstances are favourable or unfavourable, and whether the psalm is a lament, a cry for vengeance or, as here, an outpouring of praise and thanksgiving.

The second part of the psalm begins with a warning: 'O that today you would listen to his voice: "Harden not your hearts…"' (v.8). The psalmist goes on to remind his readers of the time when the Israelites had tested God in the desert, arguing with Moses and complaining about a lack of water (Exodus 17.1-7). The people were refusing to trust God, and the psalm ends bleakly and angrily, with God vowing that his people 'shall not enter into my rest' (v.11).

What do we think of this? Do we really worship a God who lashes out in anger whenever his children's human frailty gets the better of them? I don't believe so. Rather, we are again being invited – if somewhat dramatically! – to trust God first, rather than as a last resort. We know that when we strike out on our own without prayer, our plans often collapse around us. There is a profound truth at work here: when our primary trust is in God, we are promised 'the peace of God, which surpasses all understanding' (Philippians 4.7). When we persist in going our own way, that peace inevitably eludes us.

Reflection by **Barbara Mosse**

Refrain: *Come, let us worship and bow down.*

Prayer: *Lord God, the maker of all,
as we bow down in praise this day,
make us attentive to your voice
and do not test us beyond our enduring;
through Jesus Christ our Lord.*

PSALM 95

Psalm 96

**Sing to the Lord a new song;
sing to the Lord, all the earth.**

'For he comes ...' (v.13)

The 'new song' is to sound not only from the lips of Israel and not only from the voice of all the nations, but even from the skies and seas, the fields and the trees. The whole of creation is summoned to praise God's glory and proclaim God's power.

Yes, there is something of an order, an imperative about all of this. We are to honour God because every other object of worship is an idol, a non-entity. We are to worship God because God is the creator to whom everything on earth owes its being.

But the new song that is to resound throughout creation is the song of freedom – the glorious freedom of the children of God that beckons the whole of creation to break free of its captivity and to rise to its full stature (Romans 8.18-23). We sing not because of a philosophical logic or a religious duty but because 'he comes'. God comes 'to judge the earth' and does so with 'righteousness' and 'truth' (v.13). God comes to put right all that is wrong and to make right all that is damaged.

God comes to save and we sing the song of salvation – the song of a people transformed by the beauty of God's holiness. It is a song that will transfix the nations. It is the anthem of creation.

Reflection by **Christopher Cocksworth**

Refrain: *O worship the Lord in the beauty of holiness.*

Prayer: *Lord God, you draw us by your beauty
and transform us by your holiness;
let our worship echo all creation's praise
and declare your glory to the nations;
through Jesus Christ our Lord.*

PSALM 96

The Lord is king: let the earth rejoice;
let the multitude of the isles be glad.

'... those who make their boast in worthless idols' (v.7, NRSV)

I doubt that many people reading this have a worthless idol in their house, or bow down to graven images. But the psalm can be read metaphorically as much as it can literally. Our English word 'greed' can be traced back to early Saxon times. All the word means is 'desire' or 'hunger', but one that has become a craving. The word suggests that the very things we long to consume may, instead, consume us. This is, after all, the genesis of those early folk fables – like that of Midas, who longs for wealth beyond compare, such that all he touches will turn to gold.

Such stories easily translate: today it may be the company or corporation that longs for global dominion; the body that longs for the top international accolade; the person that longs for a position or recognition. Such things can be fine to aspire to. But in excess, the greed that they produce corrupts all other relationships, and distorts our humanity and society. The psalm says all this will melt before God; the dross will be consumed in the fire.

So like Midas, be careful what you long for. What we most desire to possess actually may become our possessor; our object of idolization and worship. We can be trapped by unconstrained desire; by hunger that has no discipline. It imprisons us. There can also be such a thing as spiritual greed, or even a kind of distorted Christian greed – a desire for knowledge that leads to false elevation and draws us away from wisdom. Strive first for the kingdom of God and its righteousness, says Jesus (Matthew 6.33). And don't seek to possess anything; rather, let God possess you.

Reflection by **Martyn Percy**

Refrain: *You, Lord, are most high over all the earth.*

Prayer: *Most high and holy God,*
enthroned in fire and light,
burn away the dross of our lives
and kindle in us the fire of your love,
that our lives may reveal the light and life
we find in your Son, our Lord Jesus Christ.

PSALM 97

Psalm 98

Sing to the Lord a new song,
for he has done marvellous things.

'He has remembered' (v.4)

The psalmist's voice is not enough. God needs to be praised with a great deal more volume. The community gathered for worship is urged to join their voices to the song, then all the people of the earth must add their musical instruments. But even that does not produce enough sound. The natural world is needed, too – the roar of the waves, the rush of river water, the echoing of the hills.

What is all the excitement about? God has remembered. When God makes a promise to protect his people from their enemies, one might expect that would be enough. But if we have read Psalm 89, for example, we know that there can be some doubt about when and how God will deliver on his promises. But now God has remembered, and has been faithful. Victory has been won.

But there is more. The whole earth joins in the praises, because the whole earth will be subject to God's just reign. Past experience of God's faithfulness leads the psalmist and the community to hope for the final fulfilment of all God's promises.

The praise is exuberant, because God deserves it. We too can rejoice in God's past and present faithfulness to us, and look forward with certain hope to God's coming reign on earth, when even the rivers and hills will shout and sing in his presence.

Reflection by **Gillian Cooper**

PSALM 98

Refrain: *The Lord has made known his salvation.*

Prayer: *Lord God, just and true,*
you make your salvation known in the sight
of the nations;
tune the song of our hearts to the music of creation
as you come among us to judge the earth;
through our Saviour Jesus Christ.

**The Lord is king: let the peoples tremble;
he is enthroned upon the cherubim: let the earth shake.**

'... the Lord our God is holy' (v.3)

Holiness isn't what it used to be. Generations before us were very conscious of the gap between themselves and a holy God. Now, not only are we encouraged to stand tall in any company, but God has been removed from many people's company anyway. Consequently, holiness is ascribed to all sorts of idols, such as wealth, power, sex and celebrity. Humankind has to have something to worship.

The psalmist will have none of it. Holiness belongs only and absolutely to God. 'The Lord is king: let the peoples tremble' (v.1). Three times the psalm breaks out with the cry that the Lord is holy. We have to imagine that it's the great annual festival when the rituals have represented God ascending in triumph to his throne (v.1). God's presence shines out from the Temple as a 'mighty king, who loves justice' (v.4), who establishes equity and gives forgiveness, but who also 'avenges wrongdoing' (v.8, NRSV). Holiness is double edged, both beautiful and terrible.

Our culture has lost something precious in levelling everything down to our own playground where we either play in the sand or fight for control of it. It is far better to know ourselves to be part of a moral universe with a God of inexhaustible grace who always seeks our flourishing. There are lines in the sand, boundaries to keep us safe. But the sand is always warm.

Reflection by **John Pritchard**

Refrain: vv.5, 9

Prayer: *Lord God, mighty king,
you love justice and establish equity;
may we love justice more than gain
and mercy more than power;
through Jesus Christ our Lord.*

PSALM 99

Psalm 100

O be joyful in the Lord, all the earth;
serve the Lord with gladness
and come before his presence with a song.

'Give thanks to him and bless his name' (v.3)

Many psalms graciously give space to our toughest moments. But thankfully, there are also psalms such as Psalm 100, known as the *Jubilate* (from the Latin opening to the psalm 'Be joyful!'). It's a burst of joy, with thanksgiving, praise and blessing all tumbling out from the text.

For the psalmist, joy is not something we initiate, but rather a joining-in with the joy of the earth, which is itself full of praise to God. Our joy blends into the wider hymn of creation's praise, calling out a song from us.

The text seems to suggest that to enter into joy is a choice. The psalm is full of command: *be joyful, serve, come, know, enter, give thanks* and *bless*. Joy is something that we do as much as something that we feel. It is not the same thing as happiness, but something deeper that is not dependent upon our circumstances. Joy may indeed be present alongside, around and even within our sadnesses.

When we begin, as much as we can, to move towards joy, we may discover that it is a core element of our true nature. Embracing joy can feel like a *recovery* as much as a discovery. So imagine a joyful song – your true God-given song – sounding deep within you. Let that song take shape in you and sound out from you – and see how it might bring change in and around you today.

Reflection by **Ian Adams**

PSALM 100

Refrain: *The Lord is gracious; his steadfast love is everlasting.*

Prayer: *O Christ, door of the sheepfold,*
may we enter your gates with praise
and go from your courts to serve you
in the poor, the lost and the wandering,
this day and all our days.

**I will sing of faithfulness and justice;
to you, O Lord, will I sing.**

'My eyes are upon the faithful in the land' (v.9)

This psalm is voiced for a reigning ruler, and scholars believe that it was in fact part of a ritual royal proclamation, a declaration of intent by the leader of the nation. If so, then it certainly speaks into the crisis of trust and respect currently afflicting our politics, for it makes an unbreakable link between personal integrity and political probity.

First, the ruler must learn personal discipline and obedience to conscience, to walk 'with purity of heart within the walls' (v.3) of their own house, before they can consider setting a nation to rights. Then, if they are not to end up putting deceivers and hypocrites into power, they had better continue by refusing to entertain hypocritical and deceitful thoughts. Faithfulness, in the deepest and most personal sense, and justice, in the widest and most political sense, go together and are part of the same song.

It's a tall order, and looking beyond our Bibles to Westminster, it may seem an impossible ideal. Where do we even begin? But without ideals we have no hope; without vision, the people perish. And this psalm at least sets out a vision of personal integrity, which, even half kept, would be an improvement on what we have now. Where to begin? Well, we could begin, as this psalm suggests, with ourselves.

Reflection by **Malcolm Guite**

Refrain: *Blessed are those who fear the Lord.*

Prayer: *Keep us, O Lord,
in purity of heart and faithfulness to your commands,
that your servants may walk before you
in the way that is perfect;
through Jesus Christ our Lord.*

PSALM 101

Psalm 102

O Lord, hear my prayer
and let my crying come before you.

'Hide not your face from me in the day of my distress' (v.2)

This is one of seven psalms that have become known in the tradition of the Church as Penitential Psalms because they express the profound and personal suffering that comes with the recognition of sin (the others are 6, 32, 38, 51, 130 and 143). The voice of an individual penitent is pronounced at the beginning, but from verse 13 the perspective shifts and the subject of God's pity is not the individual so much as Zion, the city of God's people and the place of his name. Then from verse 24, the individual voice returns. Scholars think that this psalm may have been voiced by a single person, perhaps the king or a representative leader, at times of national mourning. The solo voice spoke for the many.

This insight may help us to pray with this psalm by making us aware that even the most intimate prayers represent more than our private desires and longings. The reverse it also true: our most heartfelt and private prayers are taken up into the prayer of the whole Christian Church. There is a solidarity in our faith between person and community that is countercultural in our individualistic age. The most heartfelt personal sorrow brings us into contact with universal suffering. Even our deepest griefs can be offered up to God and are taken to his heart. What counts in the end is not our faithfulness but God's.

Reflection by **Angela Tilby**

Refrain: *My help comes from the Lord.*

Prayer: *Have pity on our frailty, O God,*
and in the hour of our death
cast us not away as clothing that is worn,
for you are our eternal refuge;
through Jesus Christ our Lord.

Bless the Lord, O my soul,
and all that is within me bless his holy name.

'The Lord is full of compassion and mercy ...
slow to anger and of great kindness' (v.8)

Today's psalm might be said to come straight from the pages of the New Testament – even more specifically, from the Gospels themselves. The psalm, simply stated, reminds us that God does not deal with us as we are, or as we might deserve. He meets us with love, compassion and tenderness. Always. The steadfast love of God – to use the NRSV translation of the phrase in v.8 – is ever new, and it is unfailing. Jesus – as he often does – meets everyone with compassion. In the mission of the kingdom of God, which Jesus ushers in, we all stand before God in need. We are met as we are, and with mercy, grace, tenderness and compassion. Jesus is the body language of God.

Just as the psalmist can confidently proclaim that the Lord is merciful and gracious, and abounding in steadfast love, so are we invited to live our lives as God has lived among us. And that is why the word 'compassion' is so interesting here. Passion is sacrificial love – a love, indeed, that the lover will commit to and die for. But com-passion is not just love 'for' something or someone, but love both 'with' and 'for' that person.

God loves us enough not just to communicate his passion for humanity from a great, great distance. Rather, his love is embodied in earthy, fleshly, total human solidarity. The word made flesh is God's total love made flesh. His covenant with humanity is everlasting. And even though his throne is in heaven everlasting, he has made his home among us as one of us: com-passion for all.

Reflection by **Martyn Percy**

Refrain: *The Lord is full of compassion and mercy.*

Prayer: *Merciful Lord,*
as we come from dust and return to dust,
show us the face of our Redeemer,
that in our frailty we may bless your name
and praise you all our days;
through Jesus Christ our Lord.

PSALM 103

131

Psalm 104, vv.1-25

Bless the Lord, O my soul.
O Lord my God, how excellent is your greatness!

'The earth is filled with the fruit of your works' (v.14)

It's as if the psalm-writer has spent a year on the summit of a high mountain, and from this lofty vantage point has been looking down upon the earth, surveying the sky above, scanning the passing of time and contemplating what it means to be alive in the midst of it all. And the view in every direction is magnificent. This psalm is green – and blue and brown and red and every shade of every earth-colour. For the psalmist, everything is connected, everything is vibrant, everything is wonderful – and everything is of God!

This psalm nails the misapprehension that the earth is just the stage for human activity. Actually, it's not all about us! Rather, we human beings are participating in much greater, wider patterns of existence. But the psalm also challenges the idea that the earth is just an accident, and it pictures God as the creator, the source of all being.

In the final stanza of this section of the psalm, humanity is revealed to be just the amazing tip of an astonishing wave – the people who 'go forth to their work' (v.25) and who come home in the evening. And yet that work matters. We must play our part, doing our work, loving the earth, and so blessing God. With this psalm in our hearts and on our lips today, how might we express and enjoy our at-oneness with the earth and her creator?

Reflection by **Ian Adams**

Refrain: *I will sing to the Lord as long as I live.*

Prayer: *Creator God,*
send your Holy Spirit to renew this living world,
that the whole creation,
in its groaning and striving,
may know your loving purpose
and come to reflect your glory;
in Jesus Christ our Lord.

**O Lord, how manifold are your works!
In wisdom you have made them all;
the earth is full of your creatures.**

'... they die and return again to the dust' (v.31)

The second part of Psalm 104 suggests that – contrary to how things may seem in our short spans of attention and existence – there may be deeper and longer patterns of existence at work, way beyond our own comprehension and experience.

Of course we are naturally focused on what is before us. Yesterday is strong in memory; today is here; and tomorrow looms large. This all matters. But the psalm asks us to see our lives in a wider setting. Death and dust will continue. So will renewal. Birth, life and death – all part of God's goodness – everything is in 'due season' (v.29).

Interestingly, this longer view can actually liberate us to truly immerse ourselves in the present moment – whether that is a time of birth, of life or of death. The psalmist embraces the present moment in singing. And we too are invited into a song of praise and joy (in words and action), picking up the lines that others have sung before us. As the notes fade from some lips, they are taken up by others, who will in turn pass them on. The song is always a new song, and yet at the same time this greatest of songs will always remain the same. And the tradition surrounding Jesus – who himself experienced death, dust and ultimate renewal – teaches us that it is a song that we will sing again long after our return to dust.

Reflection by **Ian Adams**

Refrain: *I will sing to the Lord as long as I live.*

Prayer: *Creator God,
send your Holy Spirit to renew this living world,
that the whole creation,
in its groaning and striving,
may know your loving purpose
and come to reflect your glory;
in Jesus Christ our Lord.*

PSALM 104

Psalm 105

**O give thanks to the Lord and call upon his name;
make known his deeds among the peoples.**

'... seek his face continually' (v.4)

'Seek his face continually' – or in an equally good translation 'seek his face evermore'. But what does it mean to 'seek evermore'? What images does this conjure in our minds?

Perhaps a doomed quest, with an ever-receding goal. We might think of unquiet spirits condemned to roam the earth without rest because of some unreconciled wrong that can never be put right; or we might imagine some lover whose unrequited love means they must always mournfully, listlessly look for some substitute satisfaction that never fulfils.

This is not what is meant here, however. The call to seek God's face continually is based on the confidence that God continually shows his face. This is confirmed by the way that the future-orientated call ('seek evermore') is followed immediately in the psalm by a recollection of God's continuous self-bestowal in history: 'Remember the marvels he has done' (v.5). We are galvanized to seek, in part, by remembering well. This psalm gives us a portable, potted salvation history, from Abraham to the Promised Land. The reason we should seek God continually is not because we never get to our goal but because we *do* get there, and in doing so find there is always more to be found, enjoyed and transformed by – even into eternity.

Reflection by **Ben Quash**

Refrain: *Remember the marvels the Lord has done.*

Prayer: *God of our earthly pilgrimage,
feed your Easter people with the bread of heaven,
that we may hunger and thirst for righteousness
until we reach our promised land;
through Jesus Christ our Lord.*

Alleluia.
Give thanks to the Lord, for he is gracious,
for his faithfulness endures for ever.

'... he saw their adversity' (v.45)

To remember is also to re-member, to put yourself back together. In this psalm, although we think at first it's going to be a song of praise with its opening 'Alleluia', it turns out to be a narration of ancient Israel's history and tempestuous relationship with God. It does this as a confession of both the past and the present, an honest recognition that 'we have sinned like our forbears' (v.6). It's always healthy to be reminded that, although we often feel the guiltiest and least faithful of people, others got there first.

This poem of remembering the past opens with a prayer in verse 4 that God will in turn remember the poet. What becomes clear in the narrative is that our security does not rest in our fidelity towards God but in God's faithfulness towards us. This is shown later in the gospels' resurrection narratives where, in places of failure and denial, Christ returns to bring embrace and love. The psalm ends with God seeing his people's adversity (v.45) and remembering his covenant, his marriage, to them. He is not going to go back on his vows.

The very last prayer in the psalm asks to be saved and gathered up (v.48). Although the human body can often repair itself quite effectively, the soul needs to be healed from outside and the psalmist knows that, left to themselves, humans can self-destruct. God's outstretched arm, his works, his presence and his remembrance are all given as gifts for our growth and that is why the poet praises God 'from everlasting to everlasting' (v.49).

Reflection by **Mark Oakley**

Refrain: *The Lord remembered his covenant.*

Prayer: *Holy God,*
when our memories blot out your kindness
and we ignore your patient love,
remember us, re-make us,
and give to us poor sinners
the rich inheritance of Jesus Christ our Lord.

PSALM 106

Psalm 107, vv.1-22

O give thanks to the Lord, for he is gracious,
for his steadfast love endures for ever.

'He set their feet on the right way' (v.7)

This psalm is the first of a series of psalms that are known as Book Five of the psalter. Although it marks a new division, there is a striking link with the preceding psalm with its continuing sense of giving thanks, and the enduring nature of God's care.

The central part of the psalm presents different groups who have been rescued by the Lord. They are invited to give thanks for their salvation. This section contains three of the four: those who have been lost in the desert; those who are suffering in captivity; and those who have been ill because of sin. Each group's plight is described, and the means of their rescue. In each case, God is thanked, and a commitment is made to tell of God's goodness.

However we interpret this psalm in our present circumstances, there is a rich tradition of describing God's ability to set us on the right path. God is not so much a divine satellite-navigation system, as the very centre of our being. When we lose our balance, God rights us; when we lose our way, God directs our feet on the right path once more. Sometimes this is done by a gentle but persistent nudge; on other occasions, it is by a jolt that reminds us again of God's involvement in all our lives.

Reflection by **Helen-Ann Hartley**

Refrain: vv. 8-9, 15-16, 21-22

Prayer: *O living Christ,*
rescue us from foolish passion
and still the storms of our self-will;
and, as you are our anchor in this life,
so bring us to the haven you have prepared for us;
for your mercy's sake.

Those who go down to the sea in ships
and ply their trade in great waters...

'Whoever is wise will ponder these things' (v.43)

This section of Psalm 107 begins with the fourth of the groups who have been rescued from distress: seafarers caught in a great storm. Beyond that, the psalm concludes in the realm of wisdom, which provides an insightful lens through which to reflect on the very genre of the whole Psalter. In a manner that is replicated elsewhere in the biblical narrative, God is described as turning the expected into the unexpected.

Those who are considered the least are given a home, and a place to dwell. They are blessed, and the land they occupy is fruitful. Those who have previously been in positions of power and grandeur are turned into the opposite. Yet again, the inequalities of the world that make for increasing gaps between rich and poor are diminished and even eradicated.

Wisdom invites us to consider what this means in our contemporary contexts. Where are the injustices and inequalities, and what can we do about them? Wisdom observes, and we reflect; but reflection is meant to lead to action. As God is described in this psalm as active in building and planting, so we are meant to play our part in cultivating our world so that each living thing may flourish in due season. The cry of wisdom is far-reaching and profound. How will we respond?

Reflection by **Helen-Ann Hartley**

Refrain: *vv.31-32*

Prayer: *O living Christ,*
rescue us from foolish passion
and still the storms of our self-will;
and, as you are our anchor in this life,
so bring us to the haven you have prepared for us;
for your mercy's sake.

PSALM 107

Psalm 108

**My heart is ready, O God, my heart is ready;
I will sing and give you praise.**

'O grant us your help' (v.12)

C. S. Lewis says that we will spend eternity thanking God for the prayers he did not answer. God always hears our prayers. He listens to persistence with great patience. But sometimes the answer is 'no'.

Yet this psalm is a celebration of steadfastness, with the steadfastness of the heart compared and contrasted to God's steadfastness. The psalmist reminds God – as though this were needed – of his promises. The two need to be related, because if we thought the efficacy of prayer was tested and evaluated through results, we'd be foolish. Prayer is a relationship with God, in which our wills, minds and desires become slowly transformed by the one who seeks to perfect us – to become more fully the persons we are to be, made in his image. This will take time.

In the meantime, we struggle on with our foes, fretting and failures – and with our feebleness, frailty and faith. So the psalmist boldly asks for victory on the one hand, but on the other, that those whom God loves (which excludes no one) will be rescued. This prayerful psalm is simultaneously hesitant and hopeful, cautious and compelling – so like all our prayers, just a tad confused.

Yet the wider witness of scripture is that God oversees all creation through blessing, but we need the wisdom to see what he is giving as he blesses us. Prayer, then, is attuning the soul to God's heart and mind – our wisdom finding something of an echo with the wisdom that comes from above. Mature prayer is not a shopping list to place before God. It is each of us, placed before God, waiting and hoping.

Reflection by **Martyn Percy**

Refrain: *Be exalted, O God, above the heavens.*

Prayer: *In times of terror, O God,
give us boldness
to act with courage, yet with mercy,
for you rule the nations with the sword of truth;
in Jesus Christ our Lord.*

**Keep silent no longer, O God of my praise,
for the mouth of wickedness and treachery
is opened against me.**

'Though they curse, may you bless' (v.27)

There can be few worse experiences than betrayal and treachery. To find yourself being 'set against' by those you treated with kindness, falsely accused of the very offences that you stood against, is deeply destructive.

Those sorts of lies and injustices gather pace, and their effect takes on a life of its own. Accusations grow in severity. Their impact reaches across the generations, damning both children and parents. They become like a strange therapy for the accusers, allowing them to project their worst failings onto innocent people, as here they charge the psalmist with the very cursing that clothes them like a garment and has seeped, like oil, into their bones.

The danger is that they succeed and we become so twisted by our hurt that we begin to hate with their venom. The psalmist comes close to this prison of bitterness, calling for the same fate to befall his accusers as they wished upon him, but he steps back from joining their cursing to believing in God's blessing.

When others desert us, God remains faithful. When people turn against us, God stays for us. When the world condemns us, God will vindicate us. Faith in the God of justice frees us not only to pray God's blessing upon ourselves but even to seek it for those who turn against us.

Reflection by **Christopher Cocksworth**

Refrain: O Lord my God,
save me for your loving mercy's sake.

Prayer: Lord, when we are repaid with evil for good,
help us not to return evil for evil,
but to bear witness to your steadfast love,
shown in the face of your dear Son,
our Saviour Jesus Christ.

PSALM 109

Psalm 110

**The Lord said to my lord, 'Sit at my right hand,
until I make your enemies your footstool.'**

'He shall drink from the brook beside the way' (v.7)

Here we have a ritual psalm that was probably used to accompany the enthronement of the king. The opening words assure the new ruler that he is God's regent (v.1), assured of victory, and that his enthronement is a new birth (v.3), in which he will reign as a sacred monarch, defeating all his enemies and constantly renewed by the water of life (v.7). The reference to Melchizedek reinforces the priestly nature of the monarch. His role is to offer sacrifice and to intercede for his people.

The psalm is quoted in the Gospels in reports of controversies about whether Jesus was the promised Messiah. From a Christian point of view, the enthroned king clearly foreshadows Jesus. The letter to the Hebrews describes him as the high priest who has passed into the heavens and now sits on God's right hand. This psalm then articulates our worship of the risen and ascended Jesus, recognizing his majesty and judgement.

It is also a psalm to bring courage in our daily struggle with the powers of evil in the world and in ourselves. We are able to find renewal by drinking from the brook beside the way – in other words by calling on our baptism, and the living water that Christ gives to those who believe and trust in him.

Reflection by **Angela Tilby**

PSALM 110

Refrain: *The Lord is king and has put on glorious apparel.*

Prayer: *Lord Jesus, divine Son and eternal priest,
inspire us with the confidence of your final conquest
        of evil,
and grant that daily on our way
we may drink of the brook of your eternal life
and so find courage against all adversities;
for your mercy's sake.*

Alleluia.
I will give thanks to the Lord with my whole heart,
in the company of the faithful and in the congregation.

'... holy and awesome is his name' (v.9)

This is a hymn of wholehearted praise of God, focusing on God alone and his glorious ways of faithfulness, justice, gracious compassion, holy and awesome righteousness. This is an antidote to self-absorption, self-pity and anxiety.

Of course, at times we come to pray or worship burdened by the challenges and struggles of our and others' lives. It is right to bring these to God our Father, who sees all our troubles and comes with healing in his hands.

But it is also good to set all these things aside, and to thank God for all he has given us and done for us. As we do this, those other things are put into perspective. As Jesus said: 'But strive first for the kingdom of God and his righteousness, and all these things will be given to you as well' (Matthew 6.33).

You can tell a person whose life is defined by praise. Praise spills over into their life making them thankful, hopeful and loving. Above all, whatever the circumstances, they are joyful!

God's name is holy and awesome. This means that worship, listening and putting God first must be priority number one – discerning what is needful from what is pressing. As the psalmist says, 'The fear of the Lord is the beginning of wisdom' (v.10).

Take time today to stop, and simply offer your praises to God – silently or aloud – thanking him for who he is and for all his mighty acts.

Reflection by **John Sentamu**

Refrain: *The Lord is gracious and full of compassion.*

Prayer: *Gracious God, you are full of compassion;*
may we who long for your kingdom to come
rejoice to do your will
and acknowledge your power alone to save;
through Jesus Christ our Lord.

Psalm 112

Alleluia.
Blessed are those who fear the Lord
and have great delight in his commandments.

'Their heart is sustained and will not fear' (v.8)

It has sometimes been said that the most important moral document we own is our bank statement. If you want to know who I am and what I believe, look at how I use my money. Not how I *tell* myself (or you) how I spend it, but how I *actually* spend it. If my chief concern is security, I might find a large proportion goes on insurance. If my chief need is for escape, I might find a large proportion goes on restaurants or beer. My children will undoubtedly be expensive, and my parents might become so. It's no accident that money and debt are at the heart both of the Lord's Prayer and the marriage vows, and that Jesus constantly talked about it and its place in our lives.

This psalm faces these complexities head on. What it means to be 'upright' (v.4) and 'righteous' (vv.3 and 4) is spelled out in no uncertain terms. It is generosity. This seems to be both in lending (v.5) and giving (v.9). And it is closely linked to our capacity for fear (v.8). Much of what stops us being generous with our money is fear; if I enter into a financial relationship with an institution or an individual, how will I stop it? Will I lose control? Will I get embroiled in a set of relationships that I don't want?

This psalm puts it the other way round: a habit of generosity will combat that fear, and we will learn moment by moment, gift by gift, that all we have is God's.

Reflection by **Lucy Winkett**

Refrain: *The righteous will be held in everlasting remembrance.*

Prayer: *Generous God,*
save us from the meanness
that calculates its interest and hoards its earthly gain;
as we have freely received,
so may we freely give;
in the grace of Jesus Christ our Lord.

Alleluia.
Give praise, you servants of the Lord,
O praise the name of the Lord.

'From the rising of the sun to its setting' (v.3)

Psalm 113 begins a small collection known as the *'hallel'* psalms (Psalms 113-118). Their focus is suggested by the title of the collection. *Hallel* in Hebrew means simply praise. Indeed the word Hallelujah (which is translated as 'Praise the Lord') occurs regularly throughout these psalms.

The striking feature of Psalm 113 is the encouragement to constant praise of God – from the rising of the sun until its setting. We are accustomed to praising God from time to time, when we remember, but here the psalmist reminds us that the God whom we worship deserves far more praise than that.

The verb 'to praise' is connected in Hebrew with the verb 'to boast'. This connection reminds us of one of the key elements of praise – that we should boast about God, who he is and what he has done. In the general busy-ness and pressure of life, it is all too easy to forget all that God has done for us. Psalm 113 calls us to a discipline of 'boastful praise of God', to rehearse time and time again, from the rising of the sun to its setting, all that God is and all that he has done. As we do this, we will discover that we become more and more alert to what God continues to do in our world. The more we praise, the more we will discover reason to praise!

Reflection by **Paula Gooder**

Refrain: *From the rising of the sun to its setting*
let the name of the Lord be praised.

Prayer: *From the rising of the sun to its setting*
we praise your name, O Lord;
may your promise to raise the poor from the dust
and turn the fortunes of the needy upside down
be fulfilled in our time also,
as it was in your Son, Jesus Christ our Lord.

PSALM 113

Psalm 114

When Israel came out of Egypt,
the house of Jacob from a people of a strange tongue...

'When Israel came out of Egypt ...' (v.1)

One of the artful things that is asked of us in Christian discipleship is to check not only on what is going well – and what God is doing in that – but also on what is not going so well – and what God is doing in that too. This is one the great lessons of the Old Testament. God never wastes a thing. Egypt might be the place that the Israelites are rescued from, and where God's mighty victory can be celebrated, but we would do well to remember that God still used the time in Egypt to teach and form his people. Even after Egypt and wandering in the desert, there is deliverance, salvation and a new moral code to live by (the ten commandments) before a kingdom is eventually established. But there is also more exile to come. And God is in all of these.

It is tempting, sometimes, to see Egypt as a victory and the subsequent wilderness years as exile and as failure. Yet all of time falls into God's abundant purpose. Wisdom is seeing that God does amazing things in the times we might regard as wasted. He works in the wilderness and the darkness – because it is neither a wilderness or darkness to God.

The psalmist praises God for deliverance. But the psalm goes deeper. All of the earth is to fear the Lord. The God who created out of nothing can transform anything and everything. Even a tiny race of people, captive in Egypt, can be taken in hand by God, and used as a foundation for the blessing of the world.

Reflection by **Martyn Percy**

Refrain: *Tremble, O earth, at the presence of the Lord.*

Prayer: *Strike the rock of our hard hearts, O God,*
and let our tears of joy and sorrow
mould us to bear the imprint of your love,
given in Christ our risen Lord.

PSALM 114

144

**Not to us, Lord, not to us,
but to your name give the glory,
for the sake of your loving mercy and truth.**

'... their help and their shield' (vv.9,10,11)

The exuberance of Psalm 114 continues in Psalm 115, with the acknowledgement that the glory, power and victory belong to God alone.

Knowing that, the people can laugh at idols and all those who trust in them. This is not a solemn psalm. It's time to show how ridiculous it is to trust in things instead of in God. What nonsense, to rely on silver and gold! What madness to treat as gods things which human hands have manufactured – there is nothing godly about these! The idea of noses that do not smell and of throats that cannot utter a word – really! Those who make and worship idols are as powerless as the idols they have made. Here is a call to 'get real'!

Compare the impotence of idols with the power of God. Choose wisely. Choose the 'maker of heaven and earth' (v.15), who has power to help; praise him daily, unlike those who go 'down into silence' (v.17). God is high above creation, glorious, free to act as he wills and choosing to help and shield those who call upon him.

God is not a dead thing but is living and personal. Though active within the world, God is never contained or constrained by the world. Above all, you and I can know that God is alive, for as we give him the honour due his name, we find real, eternal life in him.

Jesus said, 'I came that they may have life, and have it abundantly' (John 10.10).

Reflection by **John Sentamu**

Refrain: *The Lord has been mindful of us and he will bless us.*

Prayer: *Living God,
defend us from the idols which our hearts enthrone,
that we may not go down into silence
but be raised to our heaven of heavens
in Jesus Christ our Lord.*

Psalm 116

**I love the Lord,
for he has heard the voice of my supplication.**

'I was brought very low and he saved me' (v.5)

Our translation of verse 5 says it all in words of one syllable. This is the psalm for anyone who has been brought 'low', brought even to the brink of death and then, against the odds, and by sheer grace, restored. Everything is different after that. You look at life as one who could have been dead. Each new day dawns as an unexpected bonus, and all you do that day, all you receive, and all you give, comes as a gracious and unexpected extra. Recovery after trauma is strangely liberating; there is a lightness and freedom, a sense of untramelled over-abundance, and this lovely psalm is full of it. Even if we have not come so close to death, this psalm may bless us with a helpful *memento mori*.

When you have received a grace you can't possibly repay, the specifics and calculations of debt fall away and every act is graced with gratitude. How shall I repay? 'I will lift up the cup of salvation' (v.11). Whatever temple ritual or cultic gesture that verse first pointed to, for the Christian reader now it rightly points to the mystery of that communion to which love bids us welcome. We cannot repay our host, but all we need do to make him happy is take up the cup of salvation, share the feast, sit and eat.

Reflection by **Malcolm Guite**

Refrain: *Gracious is the Lord and righteous.*

Prayer: *As we walk through the valley of the shadow of death,*
may we call upon your name,
raise the cup of salvation,
and so proclaim your death, O Lord,
until you come in glory.

**O praise the Lord, all you nations;
praise him, all you peoples.**

'For great is his steadfast love towards us' (v.2)

Psalm 117 is the shortest in the Psalter, but its two brief verses still manage to encompass the typical structure of a praise psalm: the invitation to believers to praise God, followed by the reasons why we should praise.

But today's world with its apparently endless and intractable conflicts seems to be as far away as ever from the reality of such united, universal praise. There are so many parts of the globe – and indeed our own islands – where the 'steadfast love' of the Lord goes hidden or unrecognized. So how can we pray this psalm with conviction?

There is a popular hymn by Baptist preacher and writer William Young Fullerton that recognizes our problem and responds to it very movingly. The hymn has four verses of eight lines; the first quadruplet of each beginning 'I cannot tell...', and the second 'But this I know...'. The first grouping in each verse frankly admits we can't know how God will work things out: 'I cannot tell how He will win the nations' (v.3); '...how all the lands shall worship' (v.4). But the balancing affirmations ring clear: 'But this I know, all flesh shall see his glory' (v.3); '...the skies will thrill with rapture' (v.4).

The answer to our dilemma may be simple, but it is not easy. We need to allow our faith to be stretched and deepened – to take us beyond the limits of the darkness of our present time.

Reflection by **Barbara Mosse**

Refrain: *Alleluia.*

Prayer: *Gracious God,
we praise you for your faithfulness
and pray that every nation may find your blessing
in the face of Jesus Christ our Lord.*

PSALM 117

Psalm 118, vv.1-18

O give thanks to the Lord, for he is good;
his mercy endures for ever.

'His mercy endures forever' (vv.1,2,3,4)

If you were to choose a single word to describe God, what might it be? For the writers of the Old Testament, that word would almost certainly be *hesed,* the word translated in the Common Worship Psalter as 'mercy' and in other translations as 'steadfast love'. These are good translations of the word, but they do not capture the entirety of its meaning. The word *hesed* is a word that finds its roots in the covenant between God and his people. It is a word that conveys staying faithful to the promises of the covenant in everything that you are and everything that you do. So it has resonances of loyalty, of grace, of love and of kindness. Those who displayed *hesed* were displaying their faithfulness to that covenant relationship.

The story of the Old Testament is a story of God's faithfulness to the covenant, despite his people's inability to do the same. This psalm then is about God's faithfulness through thick and thin in a very particular circumstance. The background to this psalm is a battle between the king (we don't know which one) and an enemy. Despite adverse circumstances in which the king feared defeat, he was victorious and interpreted this as a sign of God's ongoing *hesed* for his people.

The psalm invites all God's people to give thanks for all that God has done – but particularly for his steadfast love through thick and thin.

Reflection by **Paula Gooder**

Refrain: *I will give thanks to you,*
for you have become my salvation.

Prayer: *Saving God,*
open the gates of righteousness,
that your pilgrim people may enter
and be built into a living temple
on the cornerstone of our salvation,
Jesus Christ our Lord.

**Open to me the gates of righteousness,
that I may enter and give thanks to the Lord.**

'Come, O Lord, and save us we pray' (v.25)

Whether they know it or not, there are two Hebrew words that nearly all Christians know, and use regularly. The first is the word 'Hallelujah', which is used all the way through the Psalms and means 'Praise the Lord', and the second is the word 'Hosanna', which is used regularly in hymns, songs and in the liturgy. As you have read through the Psalms you might have noticed that you have never seen either word. This is because the Psalms have been translated from Hebrew, so these words, like all the other Hebrew words around them, have been translated into English.

The word Hallelujah does not occur in Psalm 118, but the word Hosanna does. Indeed Psalm 118.25 is the only place in the whole of the Old Testament where the word Hosanna occurs. It means literally 'save now'. It is interesting that this word that began as a plea has become a cry of praise. The reason why it became an expression of praise is important. Those who used the psalm after it was written were so confident that God would save them that the word became first a statement of assurance that God would answer and then an exclamation of praise. The word 'Hosanna' reminds us that God is faithful and does answer us when we call, so much so, in fact, that we might as well begin praising now.

Reflection by **Paula Gooder**

Refrain: *I will give thanks to you,
for you have become my salvation.*

Prayer: *Saving God,
open the gates of righteousness,
that your pilgrim people may enter
and be built into a living temple
on the cornerstone of our salvation,
Jesus Christ our Lord.*

PSALM 118

Psalm 119, vv.1-16

**Blessed are those whose way is pure,
who walk in the law of the Lord.**

'Blessed are you, O Lord; O teach me your statutes' (v.12)

The 119th psalm is the jewel of the Psalter, a wonderfully intricate acrostic psalm in praise of God's law. As we read and pray its first two sections, we need to suspend any suspicion of 'the law' that we have imbibed from Paul's letters. In the psalm, the law is not the enemy of grace but the fundamental expression of God's love and mercy, lighting up the whole world. This is the law as God's Torah, the order that makes the universe a cosmos rather than chaos. It includes the reliability of the physical world, the universality of justice and human conscience in all its manifestations.

Human conscience is the least reliable home for the Torah; we are prone to going astray (v. 10) and forgetting God's word (v.16), which is why there are so many expressions of penitence in this psalm. We really do need consciously to drench ourselves in the goodness of God by the habit of praise and self-examination, not because we are hopelessly guilty, but because we can only learn to inhabit God's goodness if we remember to remember it!

In some lectionaries this psalm is used in the last days of Advent. This points us towards Christ, the fulfiller of the law, and its fulfilment. He is the hidden treasure we seek in this psalm, the riches at its heart, the pearl of great price.

Reflection by **Angela Tilby**

PSALM 119

Refrain: *Teach me, O Lord, the way of your statutes.*

Prayer: *Faithful God,
let your word be the treasure of our hearts,
that we may delight in your truth
and walk in the glorious liberty of your
Son Jesus Christ.*

**O do good to your servant that I may live,
and so shall I keep your word.**

'... be gracious to me through your law' (v.29)

Psalm 119 can strike us as a very strange pieces of literature indeed: a huge, repetitive, labyrinthine love poem about the law. One of the first things we need to notice, however, is that it never in fact speaks about 'the law' in the abstract: it is always 'your law' (e.g. v.18), 'the law of the Lord' (v.1), or 'the law of your mouth' (v.72). Moreover, the Hebrew root of the word *torah*, usually translated as 'law' in English, is a verb that means to guide, to instruct, to teach. Psalm 119 is a celebration of devotion to the gracious gift of God's teaching.

Contrary to the everyday wisdom of contemporary culture, our life (vv.17,25), our truth (v.30) and our liberty (v.32) do not come from within ourselves. They are found in responding to the one who created us, and whose call comes to us as a commandment that is also an invitation to enter a relationship of intimate trust. As we say yes to that invitation, we begin to know how wonderful and how gracious God is.

Yet we also know we cannot sustain this yes to God's gracious teaching; Israel could not sustain it. Who can say: 'I have kept your testimonies' (v.22)? Who could carry from beginning to end this great song of devotion to God's word as law and grace? But there is one who can, and through him, God's *torah* made flesh among us, we can receive grace upon grace, and begin to make the song our own.

Reflection by **Jeremy Worthen**

Refrain: *Teach me, O Lord, the way of your statutes.*

Prayer: *Faithful God,
let your word be the treasure of our hearts,
that we may delight in your truth
and walk in the glorious liberty of your
Son Jesus Christ.*

Psalm 119, vv.33-56

**Teach me, O Lord, the way of your statutes
and I shall keep it to the end.**

'O give me life in your ways' (v.37)

The most basic human need is for life. Without life, we are dead. Many of the psalms celebrate the life that God gives to the world as its creator. Others also rejoice in the renewed life that God gives through his redeeming actions in the world. These verses from Psalm 119 affirm the life that comes from God's life-giving word: the word of truth that brings understanding, gives hope and, through love, liberates us to love.

It is easy for our eyes to 'gaze on vanities', to look for life where there is no real life but only a mirage of empty promises. The psalmist, knowing the beguiling power of other offers of life, prays that God will turn our eyes to his ways, ways that are righteous, ways that not only promise but deliver life.

The story of the Garden of Eden pictures humanity choosing to rely on its own discernment of good and evil. In so doing, it finds itself so estranged from the tree of life that it falls into decay and death.

The story of salvation is the drawing of humanity back into the ways of God that are made known in the word of God, the very Word that becomes flesh in Christ, living the life of God in human form, demonstrating that life is to be found only in the ways of God and calling us to walk with Christ throughout our days

Reflection by **Christopher Cocksworth**

Refrain: *My delight shall be in your commandments.*

Prayer: *God of loving mercy,
in this place of our pilgrimage
turn your laws into songs,
that we may find your promises
fulfilled in Jesus Christ our Lord.*

PSALM 119

You only are my portion, O Lord;
I have promised to keep your words.

'Before I was afflicted I went astray' (v.67)

We are well into this psalm now, right in the thick of this long meditation on God's law and its implications for life and living. It is surprising how rarely we do what the psalmist says, almost as a throw-away line in verse 59, that is, seriously 'consider our ways'. There are some moments in our lives, which we see usually in hindsight, that set us in a particular direction: a relationship, a trip abroad, a redundancy, even a conversation in a kitchen over a cup of tea. The tectonic plates shifted and the landscape began to change. But it isn't easy actively to consider our ways, to look at our feet (to use the language of verse 59) and wonder if they are pointed in the right direction.

There is an attractive sense of energy here too – no time to waste or lose – act now if you need to take a turn to the right or left. Returning, and being willing to return, a phrase often used by the psalmist, assumes that we know somehow where to return to, or to whom we belong. That can't be assumed if we are thinking that we might be lost. And even when we are 'smeared' (v.69) or 'entangled' (v.61), however that might manifest itself in our lives, our desire is to be taught and shown the path of God's commandments. It's a brave prayer and can come only after we've spent some serious time looking at our feet.

Reflection by **Lucy Winkett**

Refrain: *I know, O Lord, that your judgements are right.*

Prayer: *God our comforter,*
send your Holy Spirit
to reveal your hidden mercy
even in our failures and troubles;
for the sake of Jesus Christ our Lord.

PSALM 119

Psalm 119, vv.81-104

My soul is pining for your salvation;
I have hoped in your word.

'How sweet are your words on my tongue!' (v.103)

Psalm 119 celebrates in 176 different ways the wonder that Almighty God, the creator of heaven and earth, speaks to creation in and through the Scriptures. The truth that God makes himself known to us in written word and living Word stands at the heart of our Christian faith.

To read Psalm 119 is to be pulled into a biblical understanding of time as well as an understanding of God's word. God's word, God's promise and God's testimonies were given in the past. We meditate on them in the present. But they engender such hope within us that we long for a better future when these words and promises and testimonies will be fulfilled.

This fulfilment will bring judgement for the wicked. For the one who prays the psalm, it will bring salvation from enemies and relief from temptation. This dynamic understanding of time springs from the promises in the Scriptures, and what we read within them about God's nature and the way the world should be. It is a very different understanding of time from the cynical view that everything is getting worse or from the rose-tinted spectacles view that tells us things can only get better (or are not really as bad as they seem).

The world is not as it should be. We long for a better future. We pray: 'Your kingdom come, your will be done on earth as it is in heaven'. We practise the virtue of hope, and we rejoice in the sweetness of God's word.

Reflection by **Steven Croft**

PSALM 119

Refrain: *Give me life, O Lord, according to your word.*

Prayer: *Lord Christ,*
as we sit at your feet,
teach us your living way;
for you are our Word and Wisdom,
one God with the Father and the Holy Spirit,
now and for ever.

**Your word is a lantern to my feet
and a light upon my path.**

'I am your servant; O grant me understanding' (v.125)

If you are thinking by now that this psalm is a bit repetitive, try writing eight lines of verse on the theme of God's law, each beginning with the letter N, and marvel at the psalmist's intellectual achievement and enthusiasm for his topic. God's law is what makes the psalmist's existence possible. Far from being a restrictive code, it is a living companion, a light on the path, shining like gold. It sustains the life of God's people. It represents God's presence with them.

It is not easy, however. The psalmist lives among people who do not share his devotion; living within the boundaries of God's will is a choice he had made and must sustain. He is also aware that his knowledge is not perfect. The understanding he needs is ultimately God's gift, but it also requires human application.

So the psalmist seeks from God knowledge and understanding, but also commits himself to serious thought. We might well follow his example. It would make our lives easier if God's law for us were simple, but it is not. For us as for the psalmist, living as God's people requires understanding. It demands from us our brains as well as our hearts, application as well as love. We need the work of scholars and teachers, as well as God's inspiration. We need all the resources we can muster to enable us to live freely and joyfully as God's people.

Reflection by **Gillian Cooper**

Refrain: *O deal with your servant according to your faithful love.*

Prayer: *O God, save us from ourselves,
from double standards
and divided hearts,
and give us light and life
in Jesus Christ our Lord.*

PSALM 119

Psalm 119, vv.129-152

**Your testimonies are wonderful;
therefore my soul keeps them.**

> *'I open my mouth and draw in my breath,
> as I long for your commandments' (v.131)*

There is a rhythm of inhalation and exhalation at work in this psalm. It is testimony to the power of the Bible's imagery of God's spirit as the breath of life (and the breath of life as God's spirit). Adam became a living soul at the point when God breathed into him; the disciples receive the Holy Spirit when Jesus breathes on them. Having nursed the dying in a hospice, the distinctive and almost unearthly sound of the so-called 'death rattle' was a vivid reminder to me that life seems to make its departure from the body through the throat, in exhalation. Likewise, the first shuddering cry of a newborn infant is a reminder that a new person is here, living and *breathing*.

The rhythms of breathing are like the rhythms of *intimacy with* and *distance from* God that the whole cycle of psalms tells so truthfully. This is reciprocal relation. We take things in; we give things out. Our highest good is to take God in, and to breathe God out. What comes to us from God is light, and God's life-giving words. In this section of Psalm 119, what comes out of the psalmist are tears of sorrow at the wrongful dealings of humanity.

But then tears can give life too. They can be a way to see more clearly, surrendering falsely defended positions and opening the way to fuller understanding. 'O grant me understanding and I shall live' (v.144).

Reflection by **Ben Quash**

Refrain: *The opening of your word gives light.*

Prayer: *Lord, you are just
and your commandments are eternal;
teach us to love you with all our heart
and our neighbour as ourselves,
for the sake of Jesus Christ our Lord.*

PSALM 119

**O consider my affliction and deliver me,
for I do not forget your law.**

'Let my soul live and it shall praise you' (v.175)

Try as we may to be strong, sometimes everything seems to be against us, and we are tempted to give way to self-pity or cynicism. When we feel sorry for ourselves, we do well to follow the example of the psalmist.

First, we must remember the justice of God. In the end, in this life or not, right will prevail, and love will win through. This is the clear promise of Holy Scripture, and our hope made sure in the resurrection of Jesus of Nazareth.

Second, we must learn how to delight in what is God's way of righteousness and truth. In a world where selfishness, dishonesty, cruelty and violence often seem to have the last word, we can and must choose this totally different way, the way of justice and peace rooted in God's love. And the Holy Spirit is with us to make this possible.

Third, as we learn to love God's law, we need to be thankful and sing praises to God, with our hearts set on 'whatever is true, whatever is honourable, whatever is just, whatever is pure, whatever is pleasing, whatever is commendable' (Philippians 4.8), so that there is no room for anything else.

We won't always get it right, but we must keep close to Jesus Christ; keep close to his Body, the Church; keep close to all humankind –standing daily in the power of the Holy Spirit, at the intersection where human need and divine pity meet.

Reflection by **John Sentamu**

Refrain: *I have longed for your salvation, O Lord.*

Prayer: *God of mercy, swift to help us,
as our lips pour forth your praise,
fill our hearts with the peace you give
to those who wait for your salvation
in Jesus Christ our Lord.*

PSALM 119

Psalm 120

When I was in trouble I called to the Lord;
I called to the Lord and he answered me.

'I am for making peace' (v. 7)

'I am for making peace,' the psalmist says. More literally, the Hebrew simply means: 'I am peace'. Yet to wish the 'sharp arrows of a warrior, tempered in burning coals' (v.4) upon those who vex us with words does not sound very peaceful to our ears. Is there no room for reconciliation?

It is customary in versions of the psalms for liturgical use to omit their titles, but this is the first of the Psalms headed 'A Song of Ascents' (NRSV), the sequence finishing with Psalm 134. Many modern scholars would take that as a reference to their use in pilgrimage to Jerusalem, and there are various occasions when the city is mentioned directly. That is not the case here at the beginning, but attention falls on the word that the Israelites heard within its name: *shalom*, peace. Jerusalem is to be the city of peace.

It would not have been possible to dwell in Meshek (in modern Turkey) and in Kedar (in the Arabian desert) at the same time (v.5). The point, surely, is that both places are remote and far away from the land of Israel. There is no peace without being able to go to the source of peace, which is the presence of God. Nor can there be peace so long as human desires to wound and hurt, whether with words or weapons, remain. Those desires must die: there is no reconciliation that can accommodate them. Only by letting go of those desires can we move forward on the pilgrimage to peace.

Reflection by **Jeremy Worthen**

Refrain: *Deliver me, O Lord, from lying lips.*

Prayer: *God of consolation,*
look on us, pilgrims in a strange land;
preserve us from slander and deceit,
show us the truth
and give to our souls the peace of Christ.

**I lift up my eyes to the hills;
from where is my help to come?**

'The Lord himself watches over you' (v.5)

This psalm begins with a question. The hills are not places of respite, but are where enemy forces dwell. The psalmist expects a negative answer to the question as a reminder that it is God alone who provides safety and protection. All help comes from the Lord (v. 2). Yet the hills are part of creation, so in that sense, rightly viewed, God is present in those places where sometimes only forces of evil seem visible.

The question posed in verse 1 is answered in full by the time we reach verses 5 to 8, where God is described in terms beyond that of creator, to that of keeper, sustainer, and watcher of all our comings and goings. Where we start with a question stemming from anxiety, we end this psalm with confidence and hope. We are all, to greater and lesser extents, called to live purposeful lives that through growth and formation invite us constantly to broaden our perspectives. We are not guaranteed lives free from uncertainty and difficulty, but if we can hold a perspective that enables us to trust in God in all situations, that seems to be where this psalm is directing us.

This psalm is a profound and timeless evocation of hope beyond hope, of God's abiding vision that holds each of us in his sight, at all times.

Reflection by **Helen-Ann Hartley**

Refrain: *The Lord shall keep you from all evil.*

Prayer: *Lord, ever watchful and faithful,
we look to you to be our defence
and we lift our hearts to know your help;
through Jesus Christ our Lord.*

PSALM 121

Psalm 122

**I was glad when they said to me,
'Let us go to the house of the Lord.'**

'Peace be within your walls' (v.7)

Nothing prepares you for standing in Jerusalem. Three thousand years ago, Jewish pilgrims stood, footsore but awed, realizing that the rumours they had heard of the Temple's glittering magnificence were true.

Today the emotions of pilgrims are just as extreme, but more complex. No television image makes you ready for the beauty, the fear, the sense of history, the hatred and the profound questions about justice. It's a city that is equally precious to three of the world's religions: Judaism, Christianity and Islam. It's as though God put an intolerable strain on the city 2,000 years ago by choosing it as the place where he would be made human, and it has been tearing itself apart ever since under the strain of trying to bear that responsibility.

In the coming years, what happens to Jerusalem – and to the Israelis and Palestinians who try to make a living in the lands around it – will have an impact on everyone in the world. It is more important than ever to 'pray for the peace of Jerusalem' (v.6). And it is increasingly relevant to do so 'for my kindred and companions' sake' (v.8) because even if we live far away, we may be affected by the fallout. Many people are seeking to do harm in that region. The psalm ends with an opportunity to be people who say to the Middle East, 'I will seek to do you good' (v.9). The choice is ours.

Reflection by **Peter Graystone**

Refrain: *How lovely is your dwelling place, O Lord of hosts.*

Prayer: *God of our pilgrimage,*
bring us with joy to the eternal city
founded on the rock,
and give to our earthly cities
the peace that comes from above;
through Jesus Christ our Lord.

**To you I lift up my eyes,
to you that are enthroned in the heavens.**

'Have mercy upon us, O Lord' (v.4)

Some psalms read differently depending on whether you live in reasonable freedom in a wealthy country, or in oppressed poverty.

Those who live in comfort tend to focus on the first half of this psalm. The servanthood described here is a humility that is cheerfully accepted. It is a good thing that enriches the world with generosity. These kinds of servant can look to their master with joy, because they expect tenderness and mercy (v.3). For them the psalm is a picture of how God and humans can relate to each other when Christians are in a position to serve their neighbourhoods and their world.

Those who live under oppression tend to focus on the second half of the psalm. The servanthood described here is not humility but humiliation. It is slavery. These kinds of servant look to their master with fear. They might be trafficked, they might be bonded labourers, or they might be trapped in poverty. For them this psalm is a desperate plea for help because they have had 'more than enough of contempt' (v.4).

Christians who live in the wealthy parts of the world and those who live in poverty have the same God and the same Bible. We are inexorably linked to each other. It comes as a shock to the comfortable to realize that some think of them as scornful and arrogant (v.5). It doesn't have to be this way.

Reflection by **Peter Graystone**

Refrain: *Our eyes wait upon the Lord our God.*

Prayer: *Sovereign God, enthroned in the heavens,
look upon us with your eyes of mercy,
as we look on you with humility and love,
and fill our souls with your peace
through Jesus Christ our Lord.*

PSALM 123

Psalm 124

If the Lord himself had not been on our side,
now may Israel say...

'... over our soul would have swept the raging waters' (v.4)

Our souls are vulnerable. Although Christianity has frequently enlisted the idea of the indestructible soul, this is hardly the outlook of the Scriptures. The word we translate as 'soul' in the Old Testament might also be translated as 'life', or even just rendered by the personal pronoun: 'over *us* would have swept the raging waters'. It is who we really are, what makes us us, and it can be lost. It can be trapped for the kill (v.6), and it can be overwhelmed and swept away (v.4). These two images for the vulnerability of our soul hold together the two parts of this brief psalm.

What then threatens our soul? Furious, violent enemies. That is true, and when we pray this psalm, it is right to remember people who struggle today with enemies who would erase them from their homes, from their communities, from life itself, and to pray for God to grant them deliverance and give them courage. It is right to do so for their sake, but also for ours.

A number of modern English versions translate as 'enemies' in verse 2 what is simply the standard word for 'human beings', indeed for humanity. Humanity is divided, rising up against itself. Humanity is at war with itself; it is tearing at, eating, destroying itself (v.5). And in that war our souls are lost – or rather, they would be lost, were it not that the Lord is 'on our side' (vv.1-2). Only the maker of heaven and earth (v.7) can deliver and save our souls.

Reflection by **Jeremy Worthen**

Refrain: *Our help is in the name of the Lord.*

Prayer: *O God, maker of heaven and earth,*
you save us in the water of baptism
and by the suffering of your Son you set us free;
help us to put our trust in his victory
and to know the salvation won for us
by Jesus Christ our Lord.

Psalm 125

**Those who trust in the Lord are like Mount Zion,
which cannot be moved, but stands fast for ever.**

'As the hills stand about Jerusalem' (v.2)

It's good sometimes to take the Psalter out of doors, away from home and church, and recite it on a journey, in the midst of an open landscape. Suddenly it comes to life, and one realizes how deeply the sights and sounds that meet the wayfarer inform the psalms, as all those prayers for the right path, the firm footing, the lamp for our feet, come into their own.

So it is with this psalm. It is marked in some translations as a 'Song of Ascents', a pilgrim song, and one can imagine, at journey's end, the sight of mount Zion and the hills that stand about Jerusalem coming as a blessing on the eyes and a strength to the soul. And perhaps there is more than mere analogy. The God who made the mountains firm and enduring is stronger and more enduring than his creation, and we are made in his image. Perhaps the mountains themselves are meant to remind us of that shining and enduring inner solidity of love, which is our foundation in God. Compared with this, the present sufferings, the petty tyrannies of a passing age, all that is compassed in 'the sceptre of wickedness' (v.3), is no more than a fleeting shadow, flickering for a moment across the surface of the real mountain, which cannot be moved, but stands fast forever.

Reflection by **Malcolm Guite**

Refrain: *Glorious things are spoken of you,
Zion, city of our God.*

Prayer: *God of power,
you are strong to save
and you never fail those who trust in you;
keep us under your protection
and spread abroad your reign of peace
through Jesus Christ our Lord.*

PSALM 125

163

Psalm 126

**When the Lord restored the fortunes of Zion,
then were we like those who dream.**

'Then was our mouth filled with laughter' (v.2)

This psalm is for dreamers. The roots of this psalm are probably located in an earlier experience of exile when dreams and memories were all that had been left to the people of the psalms. But it's a psalm for all times, and one of astonishing hope arising from deep despair. It's a declaration of intent for any who dare to hope, for all who resolve to re-imagine in the face of cynicism and adversity.

Dreamers are often belittled or ignored. Reflect on how often the political debate seems to focus on what is labelled as reality, offering limited options from a menu of tough choices, squeezing out alternative possibilities and quashing dreams of a better world for all. But this psalm is for dreamers.

Note here that dreaming involves both laughter and tears, joy and 'bearing seed'. Dreamers are likely to feel life more keenly, not less. In fact, in the terms of the psalmist, the seeds of the new thing must be sown *in* the weeping time. This is not a detached other-worldly dreaming but a deeply engaged re-imagining of the world now.

So what are you dreaming of? What do you sense we are in exile from – and what might our restoration look like? Be ready to be ignored, belittled and opposed. But when you dream God's dreams you may find yourself one day coming back 'with shouts of joy'.

Reflection by **Ian Adams**

Refrain: *The Lord has indeed done great things for us.*

Prayer: *Lord, as you send rain and flowers
even to the wilderness,
renew us by your Holy Spirit,
help us to sow good seed in time of adversity
and to live to rejoice in your good harvest
of all creation;
through Jesus Christ our Lord.*

**Unless the Lord builds the house,
those who build it labour in vain.**

'... the fruit of the womb is his gift' (v.4)

For many of us, life is preoccupied with work and children. We labour in some form to put bread on the table and a roof over our heads. We labour to bring a new generation to birth and then to keep them safe and see them grow. We get up in the morning earlier than we would like, and we go to bed at night later than we ought because of the demands and deadlines of our work. We are woken in the early hours by our children when they are young and hungry. We are kept awake late into evening, and sometimes through the night, when they are older and in danger.

Working for a living and parenting children – two basic human functions – can take their toll and become a toil that grinds us down. Unless, that is, they are seen as gifts of co-creativity with the God whose work creates the world and whose love fashions life into being.

Our work becomes an opportunity to work with God to shape the world to God's design. Our parenting becomes a chance to form the children of earth more closely to the image of God. Our labour becomes a labour of divine love – the love that began its greatest work in the womb of Mary and built its finest house by the wood of the cross and the opening of the tomb

Reflection by **Christopher Cocksworth**

Refrain: *The Lord shall keep watch over your going out and your coming in.*

Prayer: *Lord, you are ever watchful
and bless us with your gifts;
as you provide for all our needs,
so help us to build only what pleases you;
through Jesus Christ our Lord.*

PSALM 127

Psalm 128

Blessed are all those who fear the Lord,
and walk in his ways.

'... your children round your table, like fresh olive branches' (v.3)

Psalms can make us flinch for different reasons. There is no violence or vengefulness in this one, but we may be struck by a lack of realism and an overly restrictive horizon. Surely it is obvious that prosperity and a happy family life do not automatically follow for 'all those who fear the Lord'? And surely God's blessing means so much more than material well-being and a wife who bears you children – not least for the world's women?

The scriptural writers know that there is no automatic causal relationship between faith in God and security in this life. Yet they will not stop asserting that God's will for us today remains what it was in the beginning: abundance – abundance of good things from the earth, and the abundance of humanity itself in filling the earth and populating its history and making it the dwelling place of the creator. This purpose of God embraces our proper needs and our proper desires as embodied creatures: for physical well-being, for home and family, for flourishing community. It does not despise them in the name of something supposedly more spiritual. But it places them within the great sweep of God's love for all creation, which is the pulsing movement of God's Spirit, and which makes its way by touching particular people, at particular times and in particular places. God's blessing 'from out of Zion' holds together that movement of the Spirit with the unique reality of our homes and families today, and our deepest hopes for them.

Reflection by **Jeremy Worthen**

Refrain: How abundant is your goodness, O Lord.

Prayer: O Christ, our true vine,
may we your branches
be ever fruitful in your service
and share your love and peace with all your children,
in the power of the Spirit and to the glory
of the Father.

'Many a time have they fought against me from my youth,'
may Israel now say...

'The ploughers ploughed upon my back' (v.3)

It is a fearsome image: people using the power of a ploughing team and its equipment to gouge bloody lines into a body, taking care to make 'their furrows long' (v.3). This is a metaphor for all kinds of oppression and violence, but is also a reminder of real acts of murderous cruelty in the past. As the pilgrims sing this 'Song of Ascents' in the holy places, they cannot forget such evils, nor be unaware of the threats that remain today from 'enemies of Zion' (v.5).

Among us who pray this psalm today, there will be people who carry memories of the atrocities of war and of careful, calculated torture. There may not be many, perhaps, in our congregations, but there will almost certainly be some there marked by the experience of serious abuse in one or more of its various forms, from childhood or vulnerable times in their adult lives.

It is a terrible heresy to teach – in effect, if not through intention – that we can only draw near to God if we will forget the wrong that has been done to us. We come to God with our wounds, or we cannot come at all. And those wounds remind us that 'enemies of Zion' remain at large. What can we do? Well, we can pray, not so much for a world in which bad things never happen, but for wicked action to be rootless and fruitless (vv.6-8). And when the service is over, we can act accordingly.

Reflection by **Jeremy Worthen**

Refrain: *The Lord ransoms the life of his servants.*

Prayer: *Jesus our redeemer,*
you bore the cut of the lash
for us and our salvation;
help us to bear our sufferings
and to share in the affliction
of all who suffer for your holy name.

PSALM 129

Psalm 130

**Out of the depths have I cried to you, O Lord;
Lord, hear my voice.**

'My soul waits for the Lord' (v.5)

Have you ever cried to God from the depths of spiritual depression almost bordering on despair? In seasons of darkness and terror not easily put into words? Whatever has taken you to that dark place of distress, crying out to God is the only thing that makes sense. Even then, crying to God may sometimes feel like shouting into a concrete bucket. Giant Despair has afflicted many of my saintly friends.

The painful reality is that sometimes we have to wait in that dark place a while.

But don't stop crying out. Stay close, and be ready. Mother Teresa said, 'Prayer is not asking. Prayer is putting oneself in the hands of God, at his disposition, and listening to his voice in the depth of our hearts.' For me, praying is like joining a godly rejoicing stream that carries you wherever it wills.

Evangelical writer Jim Wallis says: 'Hope is believing in spite of the evidence, and then watching the evidence change.'

I love the way the psalmist waits in humility and expectancy for God's deliverance, 'more than the night watch for the morning, more than the night watch for the morning' (v.6).

If like me you wake early, turn those early hours into prayer for healing, for forgiveness, for new beginnings. The light of day is surely coming. Have no fear or anxiety. God will redeem and forgive. For me, it is God's constant forgiveness of my sin that daily causes me to stand *in awe of him* as nothing else does.

Reflection by **John Sentamu**

Refrain: My soul waits for the Lord.

Prayer: Father, we commend to your faithful love
those who are crying from the depths;
help them to watch and pray
through their time of darkness,
in sure hope of the dawn of your forgiveness
and redemption;
through Jesus Christ our Lord.

**O Lord, my heart is not proud;
my eyes are not raised in haughty looks.**

'I do not occupy myself with great matters' (v.2)

At last, a psalm to give encouragement to people who find that complex theology goes right over their heads. What a delight these uncomplicated words are for anyone who has sat through a sermon thinking, 'I have no idea what you're talking about'.

It's clear, of course, that we need brilliant minds to wrestle with the deep and perplexing issues of the Christian faith. If you are one of those people, thank you! But for every one of those we also need someone who prays, as the psalmist does, 'God, you are like a mother to me, and all I want to say is, all I want to say at this moment is that I love you, I trust you, and I know you care for me'.

A profound, intellectual thought about God is matched in every way by a small, simple one. And that is my small, simple thought for today.

Reflection by **Peter Graystone**

Refrain: *O Israel, trust in the Lord.*

Prayer: *Eternal God,
calm and quieten our souls;
keep us humble and full of wonder
and trusting as we live in your love;
through Jesus Christ our Lord.*

PSALM 131

Psalm 132

**Lord, remember for David
all the hardships he endured.**

'... here will I dwell, for I have longed for her' (v.15)

This is a psalm of two matching halves: verses 1 to 10 constitute a prayer based on David's vow to God, and verses 11 to 19 a promise based on God's vow to David. There are numerous parallels in wording between them, perhaps most obviously in verses 9 (familiar from Cranmer's Morning and Evening Prayer) and 17.

Both David and God want to locate a 'resting place' (vv.8,15). David's vow leads him to hunt out the ark and bring it to Jerusalem: he finds a place for God to dwell, where all can gather in joyful worship. God's vow to David leads him to seek a habitation where 'a lantern... for my anointed' can be kept burning; God chooses a place to dwell where David's successors can be established to bring blessing to all the earth.

Augustine of Hippo, so influential for Western Christianity from his fifth-century contemporaries to the present day, read the Psalter from start to finish as the words of the whole Christ, the one who as head of the body also embraces and identifies with all its members. In Christ, our desires are lifted up to become godly, holy longings that draw us out of our sinful selves and into the presence of God. In Christ, God's word is heard as a divine, unfathomable longing to come near to us, to bless us, to clothe us with the joy of salvation. God's longing is truly for us, as our true longing is for God. And these two are united in Christ, and fulfilled in Christ, once for all and for ever.

Reflection by **Jeremy Worthen**

Refrain: *Arise, O Lord, into your resting place.*

Prayer: *Jesus, Son of David,*
make us a priestly people;
clothe us in righteousness,
make us fruitful,
and give us hearts to shout for joy in your salvation;
we pray in the power of the Spirit.

**Behold how good and pleasant it is
to dwell together in unity.**

'For there the Lord has promised his blessing' (v.5)

Singing their 'Songs of Ascents' (see p. 158), the pilgrims approach Jerusalem. The wise among them know that their stay will have its challenges. Family tensions will arise. Village conflicts will not be far from the surface. Tribal loyalties will threaten the unity of God's people. Space will be limited, food scarce and water rationed.

They could argue and fragment. It could be chaos and turn nasty. Or it could be good and pleasant. The key lies in unity, many people living as one. That would be precious, like costly oil running down the sidelocks of Aaron's uncut beard. It would be like the life-giving water that runs down from the snow-capped peak of Mount Hermon filling the rivers that flow through the land to Zion.

The blessing of God promised to his people as they come to worship in Jerusalem is a promise not to a collocation of individuals but to a collection of persons who together form a whole. In Christ, we 'have come to Mount Zion and to the city of the living God' (Hebrews 12.22) as his people in one body. We have come to worship and, in so doing, to witness to the abundance of God's blessing on reconciled humanity. That is why Jesus prays that we may be one – that the world may believe that his pilgrimage to Jerusalem tore down the walls that divide humanity in order to build a new temple fit for God, the God who is one, to dwell in (Ephesians 2.14-22).

Reflection by **Christopher Cocksworth**

Refrain: *Mercy and truth are met together,
righteousness and peace have kissed each other.*

Prayer: *Grant to your people, good Lord,
the spirit of unity,
that they may dwell together in your love,
and so bear to the world
the ointment of your healing and the dew
of your blessing;
through Jesus Christ our Lord.*

Psalm 134

**Come, bless the Lord, all you servants of the Lord,
you that by night stand in the house of the Lord.**

'Lift up your hands towards the sanctuary' (v. 2)

This is the last, and shortest, of the sequence of 'Songs of Ascents' that began with Psalm 120. Perhaps it was placed at the end for pilgrims to the temple in Jerusalem to hear, as they prepared to depart, a final call to share in the worship that never ends, day or night, and to respond with a word of blessing for the one who addressed them ('you' is singular in verse 3, but plural in verses 1-2).

This psalm will be familiar to those who regularly use the service of Night Prayer, where it has by long tradition been one of the opening psalms. As we conclude the day's round of worship, we rejoice that worship has no conclusion: it reaches across the earth, through history and into eternity, and we address our fellow worshippers on earth and in heaven, calling them to continue in the wonderful, eternal circle of blessing and being blessed.

A passage dating perhaps from the third century, in a text known to scholars as the *Apostolic Tradition*, offers an explanation of why Christians chose particular times of day for their prayers. One of these was midnight, for according to tradition 'at that hour all creation is still for a moment, to praise the Lord; stars, trees, waters stop for an instant, and all the host of angels which ministers to him praises God with the souls of the righteous in this hour.' It is a precious, holy thing to stand by night in the house of the Lord.

Reflection by **Jeremy Worthen**

Refrain: *Bless the Lord, O my soul.*

Prayer: *Guard all your household, Lord,
through the dark night of faith,
and purify the hearts of those who wait on you,
until your kingdom dawns with the
rising of your Son,
Christ, the morning star.*

Alleluia.
Praise the name of the Lord;
give praise, you servants of the Lord.

'Alleluia' (vv.1,21)

'Alleluia', the first and last word of Psalm 135, was originally a call to praise Israel's Lord. In Christian worship it has itself become an expression of praise as we sing our alleluias in our liturgies and proclaim the greatness of Israel's God of whom the psalm speaks.

The psalm calls for the people of God to give praise because 'the Lord is good' and 'above all gods'. The goodness and greatness of God were demonstrated for God's people in their deliverance from Egypt and in the gift of the Promised Land where they could dwell and become a blessing to the nations.

As followers of Christ, our praise is expanded by the greater deliverance from death by his resurrection and the ultimate gift of life in the new creation. We are, as Pope John Paul II acclaimed, 'the Easter People and alleluia is our song'.

Whatever season of the year we find ourselves in, alleluia is our song because of the good news that God gave up his beloved, his only begotten Son, that we might share in his divine life, eternally at home within the heritage of a renewed creation in which all humanity is invited to share.

As we worship the God of complete compassion who gives his life for the life of the world, and place our trust in this Lord, so we become like him, changed gradually but gloriously into the image of God. *Alleluia!*

Reflection by **Christopher Cocksworth**

Refrain: *Praise the Lord, for the Lord is good.*

Prayer: *Wise and gracious God,*
save us from the idols of our hearts
and keep us in your living presence,
that we may become a people for your praise
in Jesus Christ our Lord.

Psalm 136

**Give thanks to the Lord, for he is gracious,
for his mercy endures for ever.**

'Give thanks to the God of heaven' (v.26)

If you are reading this psalm on your own, you may be tempted after a few verses to miss out the refrain 'For his mercy endures for ever' and just read the non-repeating lines. And those lines are not to be missed, ranging in great scope from the stunning diversity of all creation to the salvation story of the people of Israel and back to the goodness of God to all creatures.

But perhaps the refrain is really the heart (and the point) of the psalm. 'For his mercy endures for ever' provides the underlying rhythm to the sound of this psalm, the joyful line of bass and drum that drives the song on. It's a refrain that reassures us that all of life – on the grand scale and in the minutiae of our daily lives – is held in God's mercy, love and grace. And that this will always be so.

So, take the refrain 'For his mercy endures for ever' with you into the next few hours. Let it form silently within you – and even on your lips. Be curious as to how this day or night may take shape as the refrain goes with you, the joyful line of bass and drum that drives on the song – a song into which you are invited to improvise your own lines of love and praise, prayer and action, compassion and creativity.

Reflection by **Ian Adams**

Refrain: *For his mercy endures for ever*

Prayer: *Remember us, O God, and shape our history,
form our inward eyes
to see the shadow of the life-giving cross
in the turbulence of our time;
for his sake who died for all,
Christ our Lord.*

**By the waters of Babylon we sat down and wept,
when we remembered Zion.**

'How shall we sing the Lord's song in a strange land?' (v.4)

This psalm asks a question that is key for all of us who are attempting to live with the tension of being both *at home* and *uneasy* in this world as it is. How can we sing a song of hope and belonging in a world that catches our breath with its beauty – but also revolts us with its cruelty?

The psalm begins with weeping for what has been lost – for home, for land and for freedom. It documents the cold cruelty of captors forcing captives to sing for their oppressors' amusement. It depicts the captives' struggle to remember their place in this world. The quest to sing the Lord's song is always demanding.

And if we needed reminding of this, the psalm ends not in joyful song but in shocking bitterness, with a terrible call for some kind of just deserts for the truly wicked. Even if this might in some way be understandable – recognize how you have felt when someone has done bad things to someone you love – we know that this is deeply wrong (and on occasion the stanza is understandably omitted from reciting of the psalm).

But perhaps it is helpful that it is here, a warning of what could emerge in us if we do not learn to sing the Lord's song in a strange land. So let's rediscover God's song of hope and belonging wherever we are today – and sing!

Reflection by **Ian Adams**

Refrain: *O pray for the peace of Jerusalem.*

Prayer: *God of our pilgrimage,
you sent your Son to our strange land
to bring us home to you;
give us your songs to sing,
that even in our exile
we may be filled with the breath of the Spirit
of Jesus Christ our Lord.*

Psalm 138

I will give thanks to you, O Lord, with my whole heart; before the gods will I sing praise to you.

'He watches over the lowly' (v.6)

It would be nice to know what God has done for the psalmist that deserves such fulsome praise, but what matters more here is what the psalm tells us about God.

God is first imagined enthroned over the other gods, and in that context he is praised, showing his superiority over them. We are then told that all the kings of the earth must praise God too. The gods, and the kings – what has God done to deserve all this? He has answered the psalmist's prayer, of course, but what really makes him stand out is that 'though the Lord be high, he watches over the lowly' (v.6). Other gods and kings pay most attention to those who have something to give in return, who are wealthy or powerful. But the God of Israel, the most majestic of them all, is interested in those who do not count in the eyes of the world. The whole Bible story, indeed, shows the way God chooses to work with the smallest, the youngest, the least powerful, the most obscure, to achieve his purposes.

This has political and social implications as well as spiritual. It is about the world in which we live. If 'the Lord shall make good his purpose' (v.8), what part is there for us to play when we have sung our praises to the God who watches over the lowly?

Reflection by **Gillian Cooper**

Refrain: *Your loving-kindness, O Lord, endures for ever.*

Prayer: *Lord our God, supreme over all things,*
look upon the humble and lowly
and put new strength into our souls
to complete your purpose for us
in Jesus Christ our Lord.

**O Lord, you have searched me out and known me;
you know my sitting down and my rising up...**

'Such knowledge is too wonderful for me' (v.5)

This psalm draws us into a mystery: I cannot know God's knowledge of me, but I can name it, wonder at it and rejoice in it.

Human beings strive to know many things: ourselves, the behaviour of others, life on earth, the boundless universe. Through knowledge, we seek to bring what is outside us into order, and what is within us to communicable expression. We seek to control – by intervening with causes and effects, and by deciding when we will share what we know, and with whom.

We are able to know in part, but we are *completely* known by God. We can, with more or less success, conceal our actions from other people, but God sees it all and knows our intention before we act, and our words before we say them. We are utterly transparent before God, and there is nothing we can do to change it. The grave (v.7), the sea (v.8) and the darkness (vv.10-11) are all associated in Scripture with that which stands against God, and our being lost in separation from God. But even when we are cut off from God, God knows us utterly.

It is a mystery that throws me off balance: I think my life is shaped by my knowledge, by its achievements and its limitations, when actually it rests on God's knowledge of me. Glimpsing that brings an end to the usual stream of words, but it also releases speech of a new kind: a flow of wonder, delight and eager (even over-eager) service. We can practise it here.

Reflection by **Jeremy Worthen**

Refrain: Search me out, O God, and know my heart.

Prayer: Creator God,
may every breath we take be for your glory,
may every footstep show you as our way,
that, trusting in your presence in this world,
we may, beyond this life, still be with you
where you are alive and reign
for ever and ever.

Psalm 140

**Deliver me, O Lord, from evildoers
and protect me from the violent,**

'... protect me from the violent' (v.4)

In the scriptures God tends to be feared not because he is powerfully angry or vengeful but because he is *real*. In the presence of his reality, our own falsity, masks and defence mechanisms are exposed for what they are. This is ultimately liberating but instantly uncomfortable. Face to face with God, we are made to ask ourselves what we have turned into.

This psalm complains about those who have turned into 'evildoers'. The author does this poetically: the Hebrew words for 'evil', 'violent', 'lips' and 'wicked' in verse 1-4 are repeated in reverse order in verses 8-11 so that the point is firmly made. Whereas those who pursue evil place themselves far from God's truth, the poet prays by stating clearly that 'You are my God' (v.6); he then asks for protection that he won't become like the evildoers and turn into what he dislikes through weakness and without even noticing.

The psalmist praises God for bringing justice to the oppressed (v.12). Those who serve God will therefore understand that a divinely created human self is most itself when not being selfish – evil, by contrast, is not only self-serving but ultimately self-destructive (v.11). Those who are 'righteous' will open their hands in gratitude (v.13) rather than clench them in aggression. By dwelling in the presence of God (v.13), they will learn to live their lives in the light, like flowers drawn by the sun.

Reflection by **Mark Oakley**

Refrain: *Keep me, O Lord, from the hands of the wicked.*

Prayer: *Glorious Saviour,*
rescue us from the subtle evils that are too strong for us,
from poisonous words and the spirit of war;
by your judgement overthrow the forces of violence,
that all the world may join to worship you
in thanksgiving and peace,
now and for ever.

**O Lord, I call to you; come to me quickly;
hear my voice when I cry to you.**

'But my eyes are turned to you, Lord God' (v.8)

It isn't our 'success' as Christians that matters; what matters is the direction of our gaze. The psalmist says that his gaze is towards God, and that seems to be the secret at the heart of faithful living. The writer of this psalm is very aware of evil crowding in on him and he's desperate not to turn towards evil (v.4) or 'let ... the oil of the unrighteous anoint my head' (v.5). He is wise enough to know that what he says is easily corrupted by the shoddy compromises and easy abuse going on around him, so he's keen that the Lord should, 'set a watch before my mouth ... and guard the door of my lips' (v.3). Things so often start to go wrong because of what we say in haste.

But we are more likely to avoid saying destructive things if our gaze is captivated by the beauty of God. Again, it's the direction of our gaze that matters. If our eyes are turned towards the tawdry trivia and negativity of so much of our culture, we'll be dragged down to the same demeaning world-view. Once, surrounded by mountains in the Annapurna Sanctuary, I saw the sun rise over ten Himalayan peaks of at least 20,000 feet in height. I was struck dumb by the splendour and the silence, and I've never been quite the same since.

What matters is what fills our gaze.

Reflection by **John Pritchard**

Refrain: *Set a watch before my mouth, O Lord.*

Prayer: *Lord God, our protector and guide,
who made us knowing both good and evil,
help us to desire all that is good,
that the offering of our lives may be acceptable to you;
through Jesus Christ our Lord.*

Psalm 142

**I cry aloud to the Lord;
to the Lord I make my supplication.**

'You are my refuge, my portion in the land of the living' (v.5)

This psalm is a heartfelt prayer to God for deliverance. In spite of its individual voice, it may well have been used at times of national disaster with an individual voice leading the prayer of the people. The cause of the sufferer's distress is not specific, and for this reason the psalm speaks to all kinds of human grief. Christians have taken it as illustrating the suffering of Christ and often use verses from it when commemorating his Passion. Its confident plea for liberation from prison looks forward to Christ's resurrection, his liberation from death.

We can also pray with it as part of our own intercessions. Oppression, loneliness, betrayal, imprisonment are all encompassed in these few verses. When we pray with this psalm, we can voice the distress of those who have no one to plead for them. In spite of the lamenting tone there is also a strong note of confidence here. The one who prays this psalm knows God can be trusted. However lonely and harassed we may be by circumstances, God remains our secure refuge and liberator. Restoration will come, and then the loneliness of suffering will be relieved by the fellowship of the faithful (v.7). Ultimately, we cannot be cut off from God's mercy and love. We are made for life, not death.

Reflection by **Angela Tilby**

PSALM 142

Refrain: *Bring my soul out of prison,
that I may give thanks to your name.*

Prayer: *God of compassion,
you regard the forsaken
and give hope to the crushed in spirit;
hear those who cry to you in distress
and bring your ransomed people to sing your glorious
       praise,
now and for ever.*

**Hear my prayer, O Lord,
and in your faithfulness give ear to my supplications.**

'My soul gasps for you like a thirsty land' (v.6)

'I falter where I firmly trod,
And falling with my weight of cares
Upon the great world's altar-stairs
That slope thro' darkness up to God.

I stretch lame hands of faith, and grope,
And gather dust and chaff ...'

These are words by Alfred, Lord Tennyson. He was writing in what these days is often rather nonchalantly described as the Victorian 'crisis of faith', but there is nothing that deserves casual treatment in the set of doubts that afflicted Tennyson and others; theirs were agonizing feelings, and still set so many of the terms for modern agnosticism and atheism. Tennyson was afflicted by the problem of natural wastage in the world: the apparent disregard by God for so many potential lives and species. His worries do not have neat answers, but they do have the sympathy of the psalmist. The psalmist shows that there is nothing new about feeling you live on a hard earth (a 'thirsty land', v.6). He too 'stretches out his hands' to God in desperation. Along with this, however, he recognizes that not only suffering but also grace is radical: not explicable by way of our usual calculations. 'Enter not into judgement ... for in your sight shall no one living be justified' (v.2).

God's ways cannot be 'justified' by calculations in our minds any more than we are 'saved by numbers': the numbers of our good deeds or our bad. The psalmist is with us in finding this challenging, but there is also hope here.

Reflection by **Ben Quash**

Refrain: *Show me, O Lord, the way that I should walk in.*

Prayer: *Jesus, our companion,
when we are driven to despair,
help us, through the friends and strangers
we encounter on our path,
to know you as our refuge,
our way, our truth and our life.*

PSALM 143

Psalm 144

Blessed be the Lord my rock,
who teaches my hands for war and my fingers for battle.

'Happy are the people whose blessing this is' (v.16)

In Daniel Hardy and David Ford's seminal *Jubilate: Theology in Praise* (1984), the authors ask a teasing question: what is the biggest or most fundamental problem facing the Church today? The biggest problem facing the Church is, apparently, 'coping with the overwhelming abundance of God…'.

The idea that we are struggling to cope with God's overwhelming abundance might come as a surprise, and possibly a shock. But this is just what Hardy and Ford want to confront us with. For at the heart of the gospel is a God who can give more than we can ask or desire. Who gives without counting the cost. And who gives in almost immeasurable portions: our cup runneth over; the nets burst; we receive a hundredfold; he comes that we should have life, and life abundant; the manna falls; the spring rises; the desert blooms. The scriptures testify to a God who blesses richly and abundantly – more than we can ask or desire. More.

The psalmist prays and gives thanks to God for this abundance of life. Although the confidence of this prayer may feel overstated to some, it is rooted in three key convictions. First, that God is the rock upon which we stand, and the fortress in which we abide. Second, that if we slip or fall, God will rescue us from the swirling waters. Third, although life may be fleeting, God is not. So, we will know the fullness of God in part in this life – but only in part. The abundance of God will be known through another kind of knowledge – 'Happy are the people who have the Lord for their God'.

Reflection by **Martyn Percy**

Refrain: *Happy are the people who have the Lord for their God.*

Prayer: *God our deliverer,*
stir our weak wills,
revive our weary spirits,
and give us the courage
to strive for the freedom of all your children,
to the praise of your glorious name.

**I will exalt you, O God my King,
and bless your name for ever and ever.**

'The Lord is loving to everyone' (v.9)

This is a gloriously all-encompassing and inclusive psalm! I love its little cascade of 'all's: *all* his creatures, *all* your works, *all* his words, *all* his deeds, *all* peoples, *all* things living, *all* who fall, *all* who call. As we come towards the climax of the Psalter and its final exultant hymns of praise, we sense a great gathering in, a gathering together, a gathering across time; one generation telling another, all of it 'gathering to a greatness' as poet Gerard Manley Hopkins says in *God's Grandeur.*

For all its inclusive vision though, this psalm still holds something of the tension of waiting, 'the eyes of all wait upon you' (v.16). For there is still the shadow, still the awareness of 'all the wicked' (v.21).

In spite of that tension, or perhaps because of it, the great music of the psalm still holds a promise at its core, a promise of inclusion that goes beyond the simple binary opposition between 'those who love the lord' and 'the wicked' in verse 21.

That promise comes fully into focus in Christ, who is slain in place of the wicked, so that in the end they too, if they choose, can find a place in the most beautiful *all* of all: '... and let *all* flesh bless his holy name forever and ever' (v.22).

Reflection by **Malcolm Guite**

Refrain: *Great is the Lord and highly to be praised.*

Prayer: *King of the universe,
you show the bright glory of your reign
in acts of mercy and enduring love;
raise the spirits of the downcast
and restore those who have fallen away,
that we may sing for ever of your love;
through Jesus Christ our Lord.*

PSALM 145

Psalm 146

Alleluia.
Praise the Lord, O my soul:
while I live will I praise the Lord.

'The Lord lifts up those who are bowed down' (v.8)

How do you know whether to trust political leaders? This psalm has a scepticism that's very recognizable at this stage of the twenty-first century. It acknowledges that, at their worst, those who hold power can betray the trust that has been placed in them (v.2).

The psalmist rejoices in the qualities of our just and eternal God. He chooses the characteristics for which he wants to praise God, showing how completely they contrast with the vilest in human leadership. Despotic leaders abuse human rights, but God is at work wherever people rise out of poverty (v.6). Tyrannical leaders hold on to power by locking up the opposition, but God is at work wherever political prisoners are set free (v.7). Racist leaders make capital out of hostility toward 'the stranger in the land', but God is at work wherever those in desperation find a refuge (v.9).

Christians believe they are watched over by the creator of all things and that he keeps his promises (v.5). This is entirely different from being ruled over by another human who shares a failing body and the prospect of death. The sure hope of those who live under oppressive regimes is that, even if they cannot remove their leader in a ballot box, that person will one day be removed in a coffin (v.3). The rule that counts is God's, and we can have confidence that it will last eternally (v.10).

Reflection by **Peter Graystone**

Refrain: *The Lord shall reign for ever.*

Prayer: *Lord of all,*
our breath and being come from you,
yet our earthly end is dust;
as you loose the bound and feed the hungry,
so bring us in your mercy through the grave and gate
of death
to the feast of eternal life,
where you reign for evermore.

Alleluia.
How good it is to make music for our God,
how joyful to honour him with praise.

'He gives the beasts their food' (v.10)

There are echoes of many familiar biblical themes here. This psalm repeats the frequent assertion that God is worthy to be praised for his own sake and not just for the blessings we receive from him (Psalms 146, 97, 81). Verses 8-10 and 16-19 recall the overriding theme of Psalm 104 in detailing God's care for his whole creation. Israel has a key role in the cosmic drama (vv.20-21), a role articulated elsewhere as 'a light to the nations' (Isaiah 49.6; see also Luke 2.32).

In reflecting on this psalm, we are again invited to allow our faith to be stretched as we seek to make it a part of our own prayer. Verse 15 doesn't sit easily alongside today's conflicts in the Middle East; there are no easy answers here and we are asked to hold to, and trust in, God's wider and deeper work through time.

Despite this, the psalm abounds with an infectious joy and appreciation for God's abundant and continuous care for his creation. As Jesus later taught, 'Look at the birds of the air; they neither sow nor reap nor gather into barns, and yet your heavenly Father feeds them' (Matthew 6.26). Christ affirms both then and now that however dark and troubled the times we live in, God's basic provision for those who reach out in trust is constant and never failing.

Reflection by **Barbara Mosse**

Refrain: *Great is our Lord and mighty in power.*

Prayer: *Compassionate God,*
as you know each star you have created,
so you know the secrets of every heart;
in your loving mercy bring to your table
all who are fearful and broken,
all who are wounded and needy,
that our hungers may be satisfied
in the city of your peace;
through Christ who is our peace.

PSALM 147

Psalm 148

Alleluia.
Praise the Lord from the heavens;
praise him in the heights.

'Alleluia' (v.1,14)

A single word can carry a lot of power. In this psalm all the praises of the cosmos, earth, creatures and people find their focus and echo in a single word that bookends the psalm – 'Alleluia'.

The word may sound strange to us now, but it's a good word. It emerges from the great story, arrives with depth of meaning from the tradition, and carries weight from its use over centuries. Of course language changes and evolves – so if there's a word, a phrase, a shout, a mark or a chord that somehow carries the joy of the earth and praise of God for you in your context, perhaps this psalm gives both permission and encouragement to use it.

The expression of our praise will no doubt differ according to who we are and our setting, but what really matters is the joining-in, responding to the sensation that the joy of the whole earth and praise of the ever-creating God can somehow find expression in our voices, in our hands, in our hearts. In any one moment all the praises of the ocean can break the surface in one wave, and all humanity's praises can sound in one word from your lips.

So what might happen if we take seriously the theme of this psalm and engage with God in a continuous cycle of creativity, love and praise – and let the spirit of 'Alleluia' loose within us today?

Reflection by **Ian Adams**

Refrain: *O praise the name of the Lord.*

Prayer: *O glorious God,*
your whole creation sings your marvellous work;
may heaven's praise so echo in our hearts
that we may be good stewards of the earth;
through Jesus Christ our Lord.

PSALM 148

Alleluia.
O sing to the Lord a new song;
sing his praise in the congregation of the faithful.

'With the praises of God ... and a two-edged sword' (v.6)

The renewing effect of God's presence is a theme that echoes throughout the psalms and the prophets. This song is new, even while God is eternal and unchanging. The references to dancing and the specific musical instruments lead us to imagine that this was a song sung in the temple during worship, but it's also incumbent upon us to look closely at the vengeful instincts of the final verses of this psalm. Is this text really encouraging the people of God to enslave others, to put them in irons and punish them? And what's more, to top all of this with more dancing and 'Alleluia'?

The cursing verses of the Psalms are some of the most troubling, and the choice is often made in worship to cut these verses if they are recited without any preaching to explore them, but to leave them in if they are being said by a community that knows itself well or in a place where these verses can be discussed. That they express recognizable human emotions and instincts is not in doubt, and as such the psalms are unsparing, and inspiringly so, in their depiction of human nature. It does seem possible however to say these verses slowly and in penitence as a confession, recognizing these vengeful desires ourselves and as an admission that this is, from time to time, how we have behaved.

Reflection by **Lucy Winkett**

Refrain: *Sound praises to the Lord, all the earth.*

Prayer: *Glorious and redeeming God,*
give us hearts to praise you all our days
and wills to reject the world's deceits,
that we may bind the evils of our age
and proclaim the good news of salvation
in Jesus Christ our Lord.

PSALM 149

Psalm 150

Alleluia.
O praise God in his holiness;
praise him in the firmament of his power.

'Let everything that has breath praise the Lord' (v.6)

It has been said that there are three ages of 'man' – youth, age, and 'you're looking wonderful'. What comes at the end – of a life, a film, a book, a piece of music – often sums up all that has gone before. And so it is with this psalm, the last in the book; it arrows in to the heart of the heart of our relationship with God, and that is necessity of praise. The Westminster Confession says that 'the chief purpose of 'man' (sic) is to worship God and enjoy him for ever'. It's in praise, worship, love and enjoyment of God that we find our fulfilment and align with our destiny.

Psalm 150 calls all creation, everything that breathes (v.6), to praise the Lord. We are to praise God in God's sanctuary, in the natural world (v.1), for what God does and has done, indeed for just being great! (v.2) And we are to praise God with everything we've got, symbolized here in the orchestra of instruments available at that time. And even if praising God seems at first to be a somewhat forced activity, focusing on the beauty and splendour of God becomes a wonderful antidote to the self-absorption and narcissism of our culture. Being captivated by God is infinitely better than being captivated by our own Facebook image.

Let God fill our vision. Praise the Lord!

Reflection by **John Pritchard**

Refrain: *Let everything that has breath praise the Lord.*

Prayer: *God of life and love,*
whose Son was victorious over sin and death,
make us alive with his life,
that the whole world may resound with your praise;
through Jesus Christ our Lord.

Reflections for Daily Prayer

If you enjoyed *Reflections on the Psalms*, why not consider enhancing your spiritual journey through the rich landscape of the Church's year with *Reflections for Daily Prayer*, the Church of England's popular daily prayer companion.

Covering Monday to Saturday each week, *Reflections for Daily Prayer* offers stimulating and accessible reflections on a Bible reading from the lectionary for *Common Worship: Morning Prayer*. Thousands of readers value the creative insights, scholarship and pastoral wisdom offered by our team of experienced writers.

Each day includes:

- full lectionary details for Morning Prayer
- a reflection on one of the Bible readings
- a Collect for the day.

This book also contains:

- a simple form of Morning Prayer, with seasonal variations, for use throughout the year
- a short form of Night Prayer (also known as Compline)
- a guide to the practice of daily prayer by John Pritchard
- a simple introduction to contemplative reading of the Bible from Stephen Cottrell.

Each annual volume contains reflections for an entire year starting in Advent and is published each year in the preceding May.

For more information about *Reflections for Daily Prayer*, visit our website:
www.dailyprayer.org.uk

Reflections for Daily Prayer
App

Make Bible study and reflection a part of your routine wherever you go with the Reflections for Daily Prayer App for Apple and Android devices.

Download the app for free from the App Store (Apple devices) or Google Play (Android devices) and receive a week's worth of reflections free. Then purchase a monthly, three-monthly or annual subscription to receive up-to-date content.